COOKING
SOLO

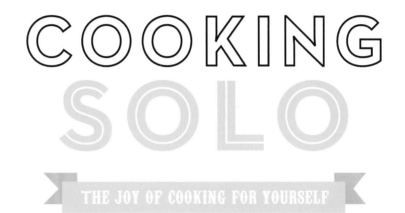

COOKING SOLO

THE JOY OF COOKING FOR YOURSELF

KLANCY MILLER

photographs by Tara Donne

HOUGHTON MIFFLIN HARCOURT

Boston   New York

For information about permission to reproduce selections from
this book, write to trade.permissions@hmhco.com or to Permissions,
Houghton Mifflin Harcourt Publishing Company, 3 Park Avenue,
19th Floor, New York, New York 10016.

hmhbooks.com

Library of Congress Cataloging-Publication Data

Miller, Klancy.

Cooking solo : the joy of cooking for yourself (and sometimes a few
friends too) / Klancy Miller ; photographs by Tara Donne.

pages cm
ISBN 978-0-544-17648-5 (trade paper) — ISBN 978-0-544-17650-8 (ebook)
1. Cooking for one. 2. Quick and easy cooking. I. Donne, Tara. II. Title.
TX833.5.M5445 2016
641.5'611—dc23
2015015219

Design by Kara Plikaitis

Printed in China
C&C 10 9 8 7 6 5 4
4500813431

THIS BOOK IS DEDICATED TO MY
PARENTS, ROSE AND ISAAC MILLER,
FOR TEACHING ME THE JOY OF LIVING
AND EATING WELL.

CONTENTS

ACKNOWLEDGMENTS

Creating this cookbook has been a long labor of love, sometimes solitary but, fortunately, more often a group effort. I am deeply grateful to each person who made *Cooking Solo* a reality and to everyone who has supported me along the way.

To my mom and dad, Rose and Isaac Miller, thank you for your love, constant cheerleading, and recipe testing. I love you.

To Justin Schwartz, thank you for your generosity, expertise, patience, and excellent taste, and for giving me the opportunity and time to do my best. I'm lucky to learn about the art of cookbooks and publishing from you.

To Jane Dystel, thank you for your persistence, careful guidance, and diplomacy, and for introducing me to Kathy Martin.

To Miriam Goderich, thank you for walking me through the contracts and answering questions, and for your thoughtful notes on early iterations of my manuscript.

To Kathy Martin, you helped bring out the best in this book and I am eternally grateful for all of your work. Thank you for your enthusiasm; speediness; and expert writing, editing, and cooking skills; and for helping me to make my manuscript sparkle.

To Cindy Brzostowski, thank you for your upbeat reminders, flexibility, and attention to detail, and for helping to make this cookbook a reality.

To Brittany Edwards, Rebecca Liss, Jessica Gilo, the sales and marketing team and everyone at Houghton Mifflin Harcourt involved with this project, thank you for your expertise, strategy, and vision and for helping me create this cookbook.

To Kara Plikaitis, thank you for the gorgeous design of this cookbook. I love it! To Helen Seachrist, Rachel Newborn, and Kim Kiefer, thank you for your superb layout and design work on *Cooking Solo*. I have been thrilled to see how great everything looks.

To Tara Donne, Kyle Acebo, Carrie Purcell, Monica Pierini, Martha Bernabe, and Eddie Barrera, thank you for being such talented professionals and for making the images and the shoot so beautiful. It was a treat working with you all. Tara—your photography is brilliant and I feel lucky to have your work in this book.

To Valerie Cimino, thank you for your meticulous copy editing skills.

To Lisa Homa, thank you for your thorough dessert recipe testing and for your encouraging words.

To Nicole Starling, Rozz Nash-Coulon, Claire Rodman, Robin Shulman, Mackenzie Crone, Davis Thompson-Moss, Tania Petit, Shay Mané, Jasmine Nicolas Mané, Guillermo Brown, Kathyrn Moise, Violette van Parys, Alana Quirk, Indra Davis, Dan Regan, Salamishah Tillet, Cheryl Pegues, Seiko Omori, and Tom Hall, thank you for your friendship, for cheering me on, for coming to my recipe-testing brunches, and for offering me advice and inspiration.

To Ada and Paolo Contarino, Daniela Donghia, Elisabetta Haney, and Patrick Haney, *grazie mille*. Thank you for generously hosting me in Italy—time spent with you is pure joy. You are muses for some of the recipes in this cookbook.

To Mary Stein and Rande Kaminsky, thank you for your energetic support and for keeping me together while I wrote this book.

To Marcus Samuelsson, thank you for your advice, positive energy, and good humor.

To Veronica Chambers, thank you for the best impromptu brainstorming session ever.

To Ellen Yin, thank you for letting me apprentice in Fork's kitchen—it was one of my favorite culinary experiences and a spark for this cookbook.

To Buon Italia, the Lobster Place, Fleisher's Pasture-Raised Meats, Dickson's Farmstand Meats, abcmkt, Sunrise Mart, Brooklyn Larder, Fairway Market, Murray's Cheese, Maison Kayser, Amy's Bread, Eataly, Broadway Panhandler, Sur La Table, Dean & Deluca, Williams-Sonoma, Fante's Kitchen Shop, Di Bruno Brothers, Kitchen Kapers, and Whole Foods, thank you for your quality foods and cooking tools and your amazingly helpful teams.

INTRODUCTION

Fellow singletons, we are a trend. There are more than 100 million of us in the United States, and we come in all stripes: We are women and men; students, working folks, and retirees; Millennials, Gen Xers, Baby Boomers, and members of the Medicare crowd. We are divorced, widowed, and never married.

As a happily single woman, I was delighted to read an essay in the *New York Times* a few years ago by sociologist Eric Klinenberg, author of the book *Going Solo: The Extraordinary Rise and Surprising Appeal of Living Alone*.

"More people live alone now than at any other time in history," Klinenberg wrote. "In prosperous American cities—Atlanta, Denver, Seattle, San Francisco and Minneapolis—forty percent or more of all households contain a single occupant. In Manhattan and in Washington, nearly one in two households are occupied by a single person." It gets better: "By international standards, these numbers are surprising—surprisingly low," he continued. "In Paris, the city of lovers, more than half of all households contain single people, and in socialist Stockholm, the rate tops sixty percent."

Besides being unattached, the one thing we singles have in common is that we have to eat. Let's face it: No matter how much you love to dine out, you need an occasional home-cooked meal; a steady diet of restaurant fare can ransack your wallet and ruin your waistline. This book offers solutions for anyone who wants to prepare delicious and generally healthful meals for themselves.

I've also written this book to encourage you to spend a little quality time with yourself, regardless of your age or station in life. Why bother putting effort into a meal if it's just for you? I tried crowd-sourcing an answer to that question over brunch with friends. I began by asking what they most enjoy about being on their own. "Freedom," said one. "Never having to compromise. Ever," said another. "The opportunity to have space and time to myself," added a third.

Those sentiments speak directly to the pleasure and value of cooking for yourself. You can relax because you have only yourself to please. You don't have to worry about whether someone else approves of your menu; you can eat precisely what you want. Plus, the process can be incredibly therapeutic. Turn on your favorite music. Pour yourself a glass of wine. Cut the vegetables. Sear the steak. Pretty soon you'll be in a groove, and the day's cares will begin dropping away.

Cooking Solo covers breakfast, lunch, dinner, and dessert, plus meals for entertaining. With the exception of a few desserts, the 100 recipes are within reach of anyone with basic cooking skills, and most can be put together in 30 minutes or less. They range from homey Fastest-Ever Handmade Granola (page 24) to sophisticated Roasted Salmon with Shiso and Sesame Maple Syrup (page 104), from vegan Down-Home Spicy Black-Eyed Peas and Sweet Potatoes (page 130) to meaty Mood-Boosting Rib Eye (page 77). The sweets include a simple and sublime Orange Blossom Almond Cake (page 177) and a ridiculously delicious Milk Chocolate Sorbet (page 208).

As you cook your way through this book, you will notice that many of the recipes were inspired by trips I've taken. I was a fortunate child, born to parents with a passion for travel. My globetrotting girlhood began when I was twelve years old. Japan Airlines had started flying out of Atlanta, where we lived at the time, and my mom booked a mother-daughter vacation to Kyoto, Tokyo, and Beijing. The trip was filled with memorable sights, from Japanese taxis with lace-covered seats to bicycle-clogged Chinese streets, but it was the flavors that were indelible. Even the food on the Japan Airlines flight seemed otherworldly: sweets filled with red bean paste, pancake-like confections called dorayaki, and my first cup of green tea. The trip whetted my appetite for experiencing the world through food. My folks and I ate our way through Greece, Egypt, France, England, Spain, and St. Martin, and they encouraged me to travel on my own to Sweden, Denmark, Italy, Jamaica, Senegal, Israel, Palestine, Gambia, Ethiopia, and Tahiti, among other destinations.

France was the place that stuck. I began studying French as a seventh grader at Philadelphia's Friends Select School, and, thanks to a gifted teacher named Marcia Vitiello, fell in love with the language. When I was named best foreign-language student, my mom took me to Paris as a reward, and that trip sealed the deal. I was so eager to soak up the city that I awoke before her each day to take an early morning walk around the Latin Quarter. I knew I wanted to return to France, and did so as a high-school exchange student and again during the spring semester of my junior year at Columbia University. That's when I decided I would have to live in Paris one day.

Like a lot of Gen Xers, I took my time finding a career path. After college, I went to work for the American Friends Service Committee, which fosters social justice and peace programs around the world. It was a great job (that's how I got to Tahiti), and I thought about staying in international relations, but I wasn't sure. So I made it my after-work mission to pursue other passions—from film-editing courses to dance classes—until I found my calling. I knew I loved food, so

tigious cooking schools in the world; what I didn't realize was that the city itself would be an invaluable classroom. I roamed Paris, exploring its famous food markets—from my Place d'Italie neighborhood to Le Quartier Asiatique (the Asian Quarter near Avenue de Choisy), from the marché bio (organic farmers' market) to the fancy La Grande Épicerie—learning to shop for the day, not the week. I also learned to let the market's offerings dictate my dinner menu—an ideal approach when you're cooking for one.

During my four years in Paris, I also embraced the French love of home entertaining. On an

"Tu t'aimes bien." You really love yourself.

when I read that Fork, my family's favorite Philadelphia restaurant, was looking for cooks and servers, I applied. The chef told me I was too inexperienced for a paying job but said I could get a taste of restaurant life by doing kitchen prep work on weekends. She told me something else that stuck with me: Culinary school wasn't worthwhile if I wanted to be a chef, but it was a must if I decided to pursue the exacting art of baking and dessert making. That's when it clicked: food and France. I could combine my loves and go to culinary school in Paris.

I was thrilled to be accepted at Le Cordon Bleu Paris, one of the oldest and most pres-

unusually chilly summer day, I got together with my food-loving French friends Tania, Shay, and Fabrice for a hot chocolate party, each of us making our favorite version. The four of us collaborated on brunches, themed dinner parties, and dessert nights with sweets inspired by Taillevent, where I apprenticed, and pastry from Pierre Hermé.

I didn't realize it at the time, but the inspiration for this book was born, amid sneezes and sniffles, soon after I began my studies at Le Cordon Bleu. I was having a ball eating out every day and going out every night, but when I caught a cold, all I wanted was chicken noodle soup—not an easy find in

Paris. Making that soup in my tiny kitchen—with dumplings from an Asian market in place of noodles—was the beginning of a new habit: cooking for one. Three years later, on another Paris night, I was on the phone with my boyfriend, telling him about the supper I had just made for myself: a salad of sautéed smoked duck breast with frisée, mâche, carrots, orange zest, and lardons. "*Tu t'aimes bien*," he said. "You really love yourself."

The boyfriend is long gone, but the remark has stayed with me—the idea that cooking a great meal for one is a wonderful way to nurture as well as nourish yourself. Preparing a meal for yourself is a special exercise, an unpressured act of creativity, self-care, and validation. I've cooked solo suppers while happily coupled and while in relationship droughts, and in both cases I have found it affirming. I make good food for myself because it makes me feel great—and because I deserve it. Being a single home cook does not mean slaving over a hot stove every night of your uncoupled life. It simply means you know how to create and experience pleasure for one in the kitchen and at the table.

STOCKING YOUR LARDER

"Eating alone, for me, is most often a prompt to shop. This is where self-absorption and consumerism meet—a rapt, satisfyingly convoluted pleasure."

—Nigella Lawson

I'm a natural *flâneur*—the French term for someone who loves to roam and explore on foot. When I moved back to New York from Paris, by way of Philly, strolling the city helped me discover the places that are now my favorite destinations for food (right).

If you live in a metropolitan area, you owe it to yourself to explore the local food resources. If you don't, be assured that even small-town supermarkets stock sea salt, extra-virgin olive oil, and other once hard-to-find ingredients—and that with an Internet connection and a little lead time, you can source virtually any ingredient you need. (One of my favorite online resources is lepicerie.com.)

Here's a list of basic ingredients I keep on hand, most of which are used in the recipes ahead. Consider it a starting point, and expand it based on your personal tastes and explorations. Remember that, especially for solo cooks, small quantities are best. No matter how carefully you store them, most food items will eventually lose quality, so don't buy too much at a time.

THEY INCLUDE:

For seafood:
Lobster Place in Chelsea Market
75 Ninth Ave., New York, NY 10011
lobsterplace.com

For Japanese ingredients:
Sunrise Mart
4 Stuyvesant St., New York, NY 10003

For fresh pasta:
Eataly
200 Fifth Ave., New York, NY 10010
eataly.com

For Sicilian sundried tomatoes:
Buon Italia
75 Ninth Ave., New York, NY 10011
buonitalia.com

For hard-to-find spices:
SOS Chefs
104 Ave. B, New York, NY 10009
sos-chefs.com

For the best baguettes in Manhattan:
Maison Kayser
1294 Third Ave., New York, NY 10021

For superb ginger molasses cookies:
BKLYN Larder
228 Flatbush Ave., Brooklyn, NY 11217
bklynlarder.com

Salt

Salt is so essential to cooking and baking that it belongs at the top of any shopping list. By bringing out the nuances in other flavors, it makes both sweet and savory dishes shine. There are two categories of salt: the type that is mined, which includes table salt, kosher salt, and rock salt, and the kind that is produced by evaporating seawater. Many table salts undergo iodization, the addition of the micronutrient iodine, which is necessary for normal thyroid functioning and brain development. All but two of the recipes in this book can be made successfully with table salt. (The exceptions are Mood-Boosting Rib Eye, page 77, which requires coarse salt, and Baked Donuts for Your Friends, page 186, which is best with flaky sea salt.) These are the kinds of salt I like best:

FINE SEA SALT: With its small crystals, it's what I reach for when a recipe calls for salt, and I encourage you to use it in my dishes. My favorite is the French brand La Baleine, which is available at Whole Foods Market and many supermarket chains and online retailers.

FLEUR DE SEL: Literally "flower of salt," it's made by skimming the crystals that float to the tops of salt ponds. I use this flaky sea salt in baked goods and sometimes as a finishing touch for chocolate or caramel. It's not cheap, but because you need to use so little at a time, a container lasts quite a while.

KOSHER SALT: I like using large-grain kosher salt for grilling meats and preparing marinades. Because the salt crystals are bigger, they are easier to handle. For the same reason, kosher salt is not appropriate for baking.

PINK HIMALAYAN SALT: Mined in Pakistan, this coarse salt gets its slightly pink hue from iron oxide. I use it regularly, often in place of table salt for savory and sweet recipes.

A note about measuring salt: The smallest quantity in most measuring-spoon sets is ⅛ teaspoon, and that is too much salt for a solo serving. That's why I often instruct you to use a pinch or two of salt and I encourage you to constantly taste and adjust the seasoning as you cook.

Oils

Oils are perishable, so it's important to purchase small quantities and store them away from light and heat in the cupboard. Oils that you use only occasionally are best refrigerated. (Take them out before you start cooking to allow them time to come to room temperature and reliquefy.) If, despite your best efforts, you detect a bitter, rancid aroma, toss the oil out; using it will ruin your dish. Here are the types of oil I keep on hand:

EXTRA-VIRGIN COCONUT OIL: Enjoying nutritional buzz as a healthy saturated fat with cholesterol-improving properties, coconut oil is white and hard when cold, but liquefies and becomes clear when warmed. I love its mildly sweet, nutty flavor in treats such as Chocolate Pancakes with (Oh My Gosh) Ganache (page 16) and Gluten-Free Chocolate Chip Cake (page 181). It also adds a certain *je ne sais quoi*, as the French say, to sautéed vegetables. There are many brands available; be sure to choose one labeled "extra-virgin."

EXTRA-VIRGIN OLIVE OIL: Used in nearly every recipe in this cookbook, this indispensable oil is produced in the first pressing of tree-ripened olives. Treated with neither chemicals nor heat, as are lesser grades of olive oil, it has low acidity (less than 1 percent) and a fruity taste.

I prefer extra-virgin olive oil from Italy or Greece, and I use it for everything from sautés to vinaigrettes and in baked goods. When I run out of butter, I've even been known to use it in pancake recipes.

GRAPE SEED OIL: Pressed from grape seeds, this neutral-tasting oil has a high smoke point, which makes it ideal for high-temperature cooking. I use it to sear meats.

TOASTED SESAME OIL: This nutty oil with its Asian flavor profile is great in vinaigrettes, especially when paired with ginger or soy sauce as in Summer Vacation Sesame Noodles and Sugar Snap Peas (page 127). It spoils easily and should be kept in the refrigerator.

Savory flavorings

APPLE CIDER VINEGAR: Fermented from apple cider, this vinegar smells awful, but it tastes great in vinaigrettes. My favorite brand is Bragg Organic apple cider vinegar.

BALSAMIC VINEGAR: The authentic, pricey stuff is labeled "*aceto balsamico tradizionale*" and is produced in Modena or Reggio Emilia, Italy. It's what you want when showcasing the vinegar in a dish like Photogenic Shaved Zucchini Salad (page 143), but for most of the recipes in this book, a supermarket brand such as Whole Foods' 365 Everyday Value is fine.

DIJON MUSTARD: This piquant mustard is great in vinaigrettes and, of course, on sandwiches. My favorite brands are Grey Poupon and Maille.

HOT CURRY POWDER: The blends vary, but hot curry powders generally contain turmeric, coriander, fenugreek, cumin, black pepper, ginger, fennel seeds, allspice, and cayenne. Madras and vindaloo are two varieties, but it may simply be labeled "hot" or "spicy." I use hot curry powder to enliven frittatas, omelets, rice, potatoes, and sautéed vegetables. If you are heat-averse, you may substitute mild curry powder.

PEPPERCORNS: Freshly ground pepper is almost as indispensable as salt. If you don't have a pepper mill, look for a jar of peppercorns with a built-in grinder at the supermarket.

SOY SAUCE: I like to season rice and some vegetables and vinaigrettes with soy sauce and prefer the low-sodium variety. Any brand is suitable.

Sweeteners and chocolate

COCOA POWDER: After cacao beans are harvested, dried, and roasted, they're crushed to release a liquid called chocolate liquor. After the cocoa butter is extracted from the liquor, cocoa powder is what remains. Either American-style unsweetened cocoa such as Ghirardelli or a Dutch-process brand such as Droste is fine in my recipes.

HONEY: One of nature's greatest sweeteners, honey adds depth and moistness to baked goods and beverages. My favorite type is raw tupelo honey, produced by bees that feed on the nectar of tupelo gum trees in northwestern Florida and southeastern Georgia. It has a fruity, almost buttery flavor that is like no other. Try it if you have an opportunity, but know that any type of honey will work in my recipes.

MAPLE SYRUP: If you are a fan of pancakes and waffles, as I am, you will not be caught without a bottle of maple syrup in your refrigerator. (I am, of course, talking about real maple syrup; cheap "pancake syrup" is nothing but corn syrup and brown coloring.) It's also a great sweetener for smoothies and as a substitute for simple syrup in beverages such as Mango-Nectarine-Cherry Sangria (page 189).

SEMISWEET CHOCOLATE CHIPS: You never know when you'll be overcome by the urge to bake Triple Chocolate Chip Cookies (page 203). There are many good brands to choose from.

SUGAR: Unless otherwise specified, sugar in my ingredient lists refers to granulated white sugar. I like brown sugar for some baked goods and ice creams, and prefer Wholesome Sweeteners organic light brown sugar, available at Whole Foods and through Fresh Direct and Amazon.

Grains and pasta

ARBORIO RICE: Native to northern Italy, this medium-grain rice is a must for risotto.

BASMATI RICE: An aromatic grain native to India, basmati is my favorite white rice. It's great with Soy-Lime Beef Stir-Fry (page 75) and anything with a thick sauce.

BROWN RICE: The health nut in me loves brown rice for its filling fiber and nutty flavor. The bran and germ that provide its brown color and nutritious profile also make it perishable, so it's best stored in the refrigerator or freezer.

PASTA: It's hard to beat fettuccine, linguine, or penne topped with some combination of tomato sauce, vegetables, meat (preferably bacon), and Parmesan cheese. Keep your cupboards stocked with your favorite dried pasta. Mine is De Cecco, which is sold in many supermarkets.

Flours and meals

ALL-PURPOSE FLOUR: I am a fan of King Arthur Flour organic unbleached, but any brand of all-purpose flour will work well in my recipes.

CORNMEAL: Because it makes them sturdier and less mushy, cornmeal is an essential ingredient in two of my favorite recipes, Cornbread Waffles with Jalapeños and Sun-Dried Tomatoes (page 168) and Lemony Pancakes (page 19). My favorite brand is Arrowhead Mills organic yellow cornmeal.

GLUTEN-FREE FLOUR: I don't have an issue with gluten, but I have friends who do, and I have experimented successfully with Cup4Cup gluten-free flour, which is available at Williams-Sonoma. You will need it or another brand to make Gluten-Free Chocolate Chip Cake (page 181).

QUINOA FLOUR: Made from the protein-packed "super grain" quinoa, this is a highly nutritious flour. I like to use it in a 50-50 combination with all-purpose flour in baked goods, and I give it a starring role in Sweet Potato Belgian Waffles (page 170). Bob's Red Mill organic and Ancient Harvest are two good brands.

Stock

You can't make a good soup or stew without a decent stock, and I am lucky to be able to buy excellent frozen chicken and beef stocks from neighborhood butcher shops. (If you happen to live in New York, pick up beef stock at Fleisher's Grass-Fed and Organic Meats, 192 Fifth Ave., Brooklyn, for Red Wine Beef Stew for a Cold Winter's Night, page 71.) The next best thing to making and freezing your own stock (any general-purpose cookbook will have a recipe) is to buy aseptic cartons of organic stock. In a pinch, reconstituted bouillon cubes will work.

Nuts and seeds

I always keep almonds, cashews, and pine nuts on hand for snacking and to use in salads and baked goods. Pine nuts, with their high fat content, must be refrigerated or frozen, but the rest keep well in the cupboard.

TAHINI: Made from ground sesame seeds, this thick, velvety paste lends luscious flavor to Roasted Vegetables with Tahini Vinaigrette (page 135) and Hot Pink Hummus (page 146). A spoonful adds a Middle Eastern note to savory sauces. It's available at natural food stores and well-stocked supermarkets.

Vegetables, fruit, and fungi

ONION AND GARLIC: They figure in almost every dinner I make, and have a permanent spot in my refrigerator.

SUN-DRIED TOMATOES: I like to use sun-dried tomatoes in pasta dishes, omelets, stews, and frittatas. They add a nice saltiness and earthy depth that fresh tomatoes lack. My favorite variety is from Sicily and is sold at Buon Italia in Chelsea Market or by mail order at buonitalia.com.

CAPERS: The flower buds of a Mediterranean bush, capers add a hit of umami, the savory "fifth taste," to dishes like Pasta with Kale (page 123). My favorite variety is packed in coarse sea salt. (Once you add them, you don't have to salt the dish.) You can purchase them at Italian specialty stores and Web sites including buonitalia.com. Capers in brine are more readily available and may be substituted.

DRIED SHIITAKE MUSHROOMS: Another source of instant umami, dried mushrooms figure in the Tahitian Noodle Sandwich (page 45) and are a great addition to soups, risottos, and omelets. They require only about 25 minutes to rehydrate in hot water or broth, and are available at Asian, natural food, and gourmet markets.

CITRUS: Like onions and garlic, lemons and limes are essential in my kitchen. Because I like to use the zest, I buy organic citrus.

Dairy

BUTTER: When butter is called for, use unsalted and preferably organic.

EGGS: Use large eggs, preferably organic and from free-range chickens.

PARMESAN CHEESE: A hard cow's milk cheese produced in designated provinces of Italy, Parmigiano-Reggiano is an unmatched flavor enhancer. Italian Grana Padano and American Grana-style cheeses are acceptable and more economical substitutes.

Canned fish

TUNA PACKED IN OLIVE OIL: The marquee ingredient in Pasta with Tuna (page 114), it is, of course, also great for sandwiches. I love the Spanish brand Ortiz because the tuna is flavorful, meaty, and sustainably fished.

ANCHOVIES: Another umami-rich ingredient, anchovies are great in vinaigrettes and in Let Them Eat Kale! Caesar Salad (page 137). My favorite brand, Roland, is available in supermarkets.

Freezer favorites

Consider your freezer an extension of your cupboard. In mine, you will always find chocolate ice cream for quick desserts and frozen strawberries and blueberries for smoothies.

EQUIPMENT

My recipes assume that your kitchen is equipped with basic gear—plus a few extras that will reward you with terrific dishes. Here is a list of equipment you will need to make the recipes in this book.

A WELL-SHARPENED CHEF'S KNIFE:
It's the workhorse of kitchen tools. I use mine to slice, chop, and dice almost everything. A paring knife is also good to have for peeling and trimming vegetables and fruit. Many kitchen shops sell sets that include both. My favorite brands are Global and Shun, both made in Japan. To keep your knives sharp, wash them by hand (never in the dishwasher), and store them in a knife block so the blades don't get jostled by other tools. There are plenty of knife sharpeners on the market, so purchasing one is a good option; however, my preference is to have dull knives professionally sharpened at a nearby kitchen shop. Mail-order sharpening services are another option. (Seattle Knife Sharpening is one long-established and well-reviewed service.)

BAKING PANS:
A half-sheet pan (13 by 18 inches) is endlessly useful—and two are even handier. You will also want a 5-by-9-inch loaf pan and round cake pans in two sizes, 9 inches (for La Dolce Vita Cake, page 183) and 10 inches (for Orange Blossom Almond Cake, page 177).

BLENDER:
Yes, they are indispensable for making smoothies (try my Double-Berry version, page 35), but blenders are also perfect for concocting soups (Curry-Carrot, page 121; Beet-Apple-Carrot Potage, page 125), dips and spreads (Hot Pink Hummus, page 146), nut milks (Handmade Almond Milk, page 38), juices (Emerald Elixir, page 37), and frozen desserts (Cantaloupe-Mint Sorbet, page 206).

COLANDERS:
A colander—in mesh or perforated metal or plastic—is a must for draining pasta and convenient for rinsing produce. Cuisinart and other manufacturers have a rectangular model with handles on the sides that pull out and rest on the edges of the sink, holding the food securely above the draining water.

CUTTING BOARDS: It's best to have several—one for meat, another for vegetables, a third for fish, and even one for fruit and chocolate. I like wooden cutting boards as well as plastic ones, which have the advantage of being dishwasher safe.

ELECTRIC HAND MIXER: In culinary school, we mixed almost everything with a whisk. I continue to do a lot of whisking, but I prefer an electric hand mixer for some batters (see Orange Blossom Almond Cake, page 177). An electric mixer produces a better consistency, accomplishes the task more quickly, and saves wear and tear on your arm. Plus, a hand mixer takes up less space than a stand model and costs a fraction as much. (You can get a decent one for about $25.)

MEASURING CUPS AND SPOONS: They're a must for precise measurement, which, in turn, is essential for baking. You will need a standard set of dry measures ($\frac{1}{4}$-, $\frac{1}{3}$-, $\frac{1}{2}$-, and 1-cup sizes), plus 1- and 2-cup liquid measures. The two types of cups—liquid and dry—are not interchangeable. A measuring-spoon set, however, handles both types of ingredients.

Yours should have at least six measures: $\frac{1}{8}$, $\frac{1}{4}$, $\frac{1}{2}$, and 1 teaspoon plus $\frac{1}{2}$ and 1 tablespoon. The brand POURfect makes a 12-piece set (available at amazon.com and chefscatalog.com) that takes you all the way from a $\frac{1}{64}$ teaspoon of dubious utility to a handy 2 tablespoons (equivalent to $\frac{1}{8}$ cup) and includes the elusive $\frac{1}{3}$ teaspoon.

MICROPLANE RASP GRATER: There's nothing like it for zesting citrus peel and grating hard cheese into fine shreds. Wash it by hand and slide it back into its sheath after every use so it won't lose its edge.

MIXING BOWLS: Essential for mixing, tossing, and holding ingredients, a nesting set of various size stainless steel or glass bowls will cover most kitchen contingencies and take up minimum storage space.

PANCAKE GRIDDLE: If you have the storage space and are a frequent flapjack maker, a griddle (either electric or stovetop) is the best way to cook a batch of pancakes. A $9\frac{1}{2}$-inch crêpe pan is the next best thing.

PARCHMENT PAPER: Line baking sheets with parchment when you're baking cookies or roasting vegetables and its nonstick surface will make cleanup a snap. Just don't use it under the broiler; it can't handle the intense heat and could catch fire.

RAMEKINS: I use individual ramekins for both savory and sweet dishes, from Duck Shepherd's Pie (page 90) to Parisian Mini Chestnut Cakes (page 199). You will want several 3- and 4-inch ones.

SALAD SPINNER: There are a ton of salad recipes in this cookbook, and I always rinse my greens before eating them. Salad spinners make cleaning lettuce and other greens an easy task. My favorite model is the OXO Good Grips Salad Spinner.

SHALLOW 1-QUART CASSEROLE DISH: It's a practical dish for cooking a single portion of fish or roasting vegetables.

SKILLETS: I use 6-, 8-, and 10-inch sizes, and prefer cast iron because some of my recipes call for transferring the skillet from the stovetop to the oven. If your cast iron is well seasoned (as it should be), it will be close to nonstick. (Food52.com has an excellent video on caring for cast iron, including instructions for restoring the seasoning.)

SPATULAS: There are three types of spatulas, and you will want at least two of them. A silicone or rubber spatula is used to stir and scrape batters and other loose mixtures; one is essential, and two or three, in various sizes, are convenient. You'll also need a 2½- or 3-inch-wide metal or nylon spatula for flipping burgers and pancakes. A ¾- to 1-inch-wide offset spatula is useful but not essential for icing cakes, spreading fillings, and removing cookies from a baking sheet.

TONGS: You'll be glad you have tongs whenever you have to pick up, turn, transfer, or toss hot or messy food items. (Grab them to turn the Mood Boosting Rib-Eye, page 77, and to combine Tahitian Noodles, page 45, with their dressing.) Stainless steel tongs are best, in 9½- and/or 12-inch lengths.

VEGETABLE PEELER: I use this tool to peel vegetables and fruit, and to make Photogenic Shaved Zucchini Salad (page 143). My favorite brand is OXO, and I prefer a straight blade to the serrated type.

WAFFLE IRON: Hands down, waffles are my favorite food group, in versions both sweet (Chocolate Waffles with Ganache, page 173; Pumpkin–Apple Cider Waffles, page 169) and savory (Cornbread Waffles with Jalapeños and Sun-Dried Tomatoes, page 168). In my world, they're as delicious for dinner as they are for brunch. (Try the cornbread waffles with Tarragon Roasted Chicken, page 92.) If you share my passion or are open to being smitten by waffles, there is no getting around the fact that you're going to need at least one waffle iron. I have two Cuisinart models, one for Belgian waffles, the other for standard ones.

WHISKS: They are right up there with chef's knives in the workhorse department. You will want one in your hand for everything from making omelets to whipping cream and emulsifying vinaigrettes. If you buy just one, make it a balloon whisk.

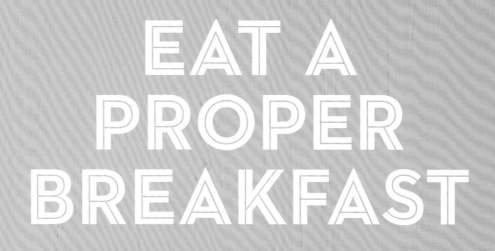

EAT A PROPER BREAKFAST

"Why, sometimes I've believed as many as six impossible things before breakfast."

—*Alice's Adventures in Wonderland* by Lewis Carroll

You never know what the day may bring, so fuel your engine first thing. That's my maxim. On a workday, that may mean a virtuous bowl of oatmeal (make it my flavor-packed Triple the Coconut Oatmeal, page 23) or a quick Double-Berry Smoothie (page 35). At least once a week, though, you deserve to pamper yourself with a leisurely and indulgent morning meal like my Chocolate Pancakes with (Oh My Gosh) Ganache (page 16) or Ginger Biscuit-Scones with Quince Compote (page 31).

I'M AN UNREPENTANT CHOCOHOLIC; in fact, some mornings I can't get going without it. For a while, I got by with a cup of hot chocolate, but then I began experimenting with pancakes. Putting my pastry training to work, I figured out that the key to producing sturdy, not mushy, chocolate hotcakes is cornmeal. It creates an almost cake-like texture that can stand up to syrup, or, in this case, ganache, an utterly decadent yet effortless sauce of heavy cream and semisweet chocolate. In the likely event that you cannot eat five pancakes in a single sitting, seal the leftovers in aluminum foil and refrigerate them. They'll reheat beautifully in 5 to 8 minutes in a toaster oven or oven preheated to 350°F. (Leave them in the foil. And don't use a microwave; it will make them rubbery.)

CHOCOLATE PANCAKES WITH (OH MY GOSH) GANACHE

MAKES 5 MEDIUM PANCAKES

½ cup finely ground yellow or white cornmeal

¼ cup all-purpose flour

¼ cup unsweetened cocoa powder

1 tablespoon light brown sugar

1½ teaspoons baking powder

⅛ teaspoon salt

¾ cup milk (preferably whole, but skim or nondairy will work)

1 large egg

3 tablespoons plus 2 teaspoons coconut oil or melted butter

¼ to ½ cup Chocolate Ganache, for serving (recipe follows)

1   In a large bowl, combine the cornmeal, flour, cocoa powder, brown sugar, baking powder, and salt. Whisk until the cocoa powder is evenly distributed. Combine the milk, egg, and 3 tablespoons of the coconut oil in a smaller bowl and whisk until mixed.

2   Pour half the liquid ingredients into the dry mixture and use a large spoon or rubber spatula to stir them together; the batter will be lumpy. Stir in the remaining liquid. Using a handheld electric mixer, beat the batter on high speed until smooth, 1 to 2 minutes.

3   Set a griddle or crêpe pan over medium-high heat. Add the remaining 2 teaspoons coconut oil to the pan, spreading it with a spatula to coat the bottom. Pour in about ⅓ cup batter for each pancake. (If using a griddle, leave about 2 inches between each portion.)

4   When the pancakes are bubbly on top and lightly browned on the bottom (after about 2 minutes), use a wide metal spatula to flip them. Cook the second side for about 2 minutes, and use the spatula to transfer the pancakes to a serving plate. Serve immediately with the Chocolate Ganache on the side for spreading.

. . . continued

HOT COCOA

I once worked at a tea salon in Paris where the bread baker showered in the kitchen. Dodgy as it was, the place taught me how to make the best hot chocolate. The secret? Chocolate ganache. Simply heat a cup of whole milk over medium heat, whisking constantly, just until it begins to boil, about 3 minutes. Lower the heat, add 1 table-spoon ganache, and whisk until the chocolate is incorporated. Pour into a mug and enjoy.

CHOCOLATE GANACHE MAKES 1½ CUPS

You could make ganache with chocolate chips (no chopping required), but it will be even better if you buy a bar of quality semisweet chocolate such as Scharffen Berger or Ghirardelli. Plan to have the chocolate chopped and the cream in the saucepan when you begin the pancake recipe so you can finish the ganache while the flapjacks cook. You'll be blessed with extra ganache, which is scrumptious spread on toast or over ice cream or fruit. You can keep it in the refrigerator for up to 5 days in a lidded container or freeze it in an airtight container for up to 2 months. If frozen, let it thaw in the refrigerator overnight. Reheat the desired amount in a small saucepan over low heat or in a microwave at full power in 15-second increments.

4 ounces semisweet chocolate

1 cup heavy whipping cream

1   With a chef's knife, coarsely chop the chocolate on a cutting board and sweep it with your hand into a medium bowl.

2   Pour the cream into a small saucepan and heat it over medium-high heat, stirring constantly, just until it begins to boil, about 3 minutes.

3   Remove the cream from the heat and pour it over the chocolate. Let it stand until the chocolate is very soft, 2 to 3 minutes. Whisk the mixture until it is smooth and homogenous.

WHAT WOULD MAKE YOU WILDLY HAPPY: winning the lottery? Falling in love? Getting a puppy? Imagine how ecstatic you'd be, and you'll know how I feel about eating pancakes. They're lovely to look at, comforting, and delicious. People, let's face it: They're basically miniature cakes you get to eat first thing in the morning. I also love lemons. Their scent and flavor are amazing in baked goods—and pancakes. This recipe calls for lemon extract, which is essentially oil extracted from lemon peel. (Think of it as the citrus equivalent of vanilla extract.) My favorite brand is Frontier Co-op, available at Whole Foods; they have an organic lemon flavor and a conventional lemon flavor. That's also where you'll find quinoa flour, which gives these hearty flapjacks a protein boost. If you don't have time for a trip to the store, you can substitute lemon zest for the flavoring and all-purpose flour for the quinoa. This is a thick batter, so use your spatula to flatten the pancakes while they cook. If you would like thinner pancakes, add 2 or more tablespoons of milk to the batter. As with the Chocolate Pancakes (page 16), any extras can be refrigerated or frozen and reheated. If you're especially ravenous, these pancakes pair beautifully with the Goji Berry Fruit Salad on page 33.

LEMONY PANCAKES (A LOVE STORY)

MAKES 5 MEDIUM PANCAKES

1 In a large bowl, combine the cornmeal, quinoa flour, sugar, baking powder, and salt. Whisk to combine. In a small bowl, whisk the milk with the egg, 3 tablespoons of the butter, and the lemon extract until mixed.

. . . *continued*

½ cup finely ground yellow cornmeal

½ cup quinoa flour

1 tablespoon sugar

1½ teaspoons baking powder

¼ teaspoon salt

½ cup milk (preferably whole, but skim or nondairy will work)

1 large egg

3 tablespoons butter, melted, plus 2 teaspoons for the pan

1 teaspoon lemon extract or the finely grated zest of 1 lemon

Maple syrup, for serving

2 Pour half the liquid ingredients into the dry mixture and use a large spoon or rubber spatula to stir them together; the batter will be lumpy. Stir in the remaining liquid. Using a handheld electric mixer, beat the batter on high speed until smooth, 1 to 2 minutes.

3 Place a griddle or crêpe pan over medium-high heat. Add the remaining 2 teaspoons butter, spreading it to coat the pan. Working in batches if necessary, pour in about ⅓ cup batter for each pancake. (If using a griddle, leave about 2 inches between each portion.)

4 When the top is bubbly and the bottom is golden brown (after about 2 minutes), flip the pancakes with a wide metal spatula and gently flatten them with the back of the spatula. Cook until golden brown on the second side, about 2 minutes. Use the spatula to transfer them to a serving plate, and serve immediately with maple syrup.

AH, OATMEAL—THE UGLY SIBLING of every breakfast option. Who grows up actually liking the stuff? As a kid, I wanted colorful, super-sweet Froot Loops (never got them unless I slept over at a friend's house). Today I know that what oatmeal lacks in looks it makes up for in cholesterol-lowering soluble fiber and that stick-to-your-ribs quality every first meal should have. I've learned to like oatmeal by dressing it up with granola, chopped dates, dark chocolate, or all of the above. This recipe adds coconut in three forms for nuttiness and a hint of sweetness.

TRIPLE THE COCONUT OATMEAL

MAKES 1 SERVING

½ cup water

½ cup coconut milk

½ cup old-fashioned rolled oats

2 teaspoons coconut oil

Salt

1 teaspoon unsweetened coconut flakes

1 teaspoon maple syrup or other sweetener (optional)

1 tablespoon granola (preferably homemade; recipe follows), chopped semisweet chocolate, and/or chopped dates (optional)

1 In a small saucepan, bring the water and coconut milk to a boil over high heat. Add the oats, decrease the heat to low, and stir in the coconut oil and a pinch of salt. Simmer, stirring occasionally, until the oatmeal is thick, about 5 minutes.

2 Transfer the oatmeal to a bowl, sprinkle it with the coconut flakes, and top with the maple syrup and the granola, chocolate and/or dates, if desired. Serve immediately.

I BEGAN MAKING MY OWN GRANOLA after buying one too many bags of the stale stuff. It turns out granola is easy to prepare—just dump, stir, and bake. Some people roast the oats for a long period of time at a low temperature. I'm impatient, so I put everything in the oven at 400°F, and pull out freshly roasted granola after 10 or 15 minutes. You have to pay attention (your nose will know), or the cherries will burn and the oats will get too dark and taste bitter. The recipe makes enough for several breakfasts, and it will keep well at room temperature for up to a week. I like to eat it with almond milk, over yogurt, or sprinkled on top of oatmeal.

FASTEST-EVER HANDMADE GRANOLA

MAKES 3 OR 4 SERVINGS

1 cup old-fashioned rolled oats

½ cup dried cherries, chopped

½ cup Medjool dates, chopped

1 tablespoon coconut oil

1 tablespoon maple syrup

1 teaspoon ground cinnamon

¼ teaspoon salt (preferably fleur de sel or other flaky sea salt)

1 Preheat the oven to 400°F.

2 In a large bowl, combine the oats, cherries, dates, coconut oil, maple syrup, cinnamon, and salt, mixing well with your hands. Line a baking sheet with parchment paper and spread the mixture onto it.

3 Place the pan in the oven, and let the granola bake for 10 to 15 minutes, until it's fragrant and light golden brown. Let it cool to room temperature before transferring to a mason jar or other airtight container.

WHEN I TRIED TO MAKE a frittata for one, it came out of the oven puffed up like a soufflé—a happy accident that is more artful than your average breakfast. If you're a morning person, you can prepare the ingredients first thing, pop the frittata-soufflé into the oven, and sit down to eat when you get out of the shower. If, like me, you're not an early riser, this makes a great weekend breakfast—especially with Rosemary-Cheddar Buttermilk Biscuits (page 175).

FRITTATA-SOUFFLÉ FOR ONE

MAKES 1 SERVING

2 large eggs

¼ cup heavy whipping cream

Salt

Freshly ground black pepper

½ teaspoon extra-virgin olive oil

4 cherry tomatoes, halved

½ teaspoon chopped fresh cilantro (optional)

1   Preheat the oven to 400°F.

2   Break the eggs into a medium bowl. Add the cream, a pinch of salt, and a grind of pepper, and whisk until the ingredients are well combined.

3   Pour the olive oil into a 4-inch ramekin, turning it to coat the bottom and sides. Add the tomatoes and cilantro, if desired, and pour the egg mixture on top.

4   Put the ramekin on a baking sheet and place it in the oven to cook for 20 minutes, or until set and puffed. Let it cool for a few minutes before serving.

I WAS MAKING BRUNCH for a vegetarian friend and thought it would be fun to have tacos, so I used eggs instead of my usual fish, and I fell in love with this variation. Because the eggs are the stars here, you'll want to buy the best you can find—ideally at a farmers' market. You'll also want to use a nonstick skillet so the eggs can be easily removed from the pan.

SUNNY-SIDE-UP TACO MAKES 1 SERVING

2 (6-inch) corn tortillas

1 tablespoon extra-virgin olive oil

2 large eggs

Salt

Guacamole for One (page 80)

Pico de Gallo for One (page 79)

½ lime, cut into quarters

1 In a small cast-iron skillet over low heat, warm the tortillas, turning once, for about 2 minutes per side. Remove the pan from the heat.

2 Heat the olive oil in a small nonstick skillet over medium-high heat, tilting the pan to coat the bottom.

3 Crack the eggs into a small bowl, slip them into the pan, and immediately decrease the heat to low. Let the eggs cook, without turning, until the whites are set and the yolks are as firm as you like them, 4 to 6 minutes. Sprinkle with a pinch of salt.

4 Arrange the tortillas, slightly overlapping, on a serving plate and spread with the guacamole. Use a wide metal spatula to place the eggs on the tortillas. Top with the pico de gallo, squirt with lime juice, and serve.

IT'S BEEN SAID THAT you can judge a chef by his or her ability to make an omelet. I couldn't care less; what interests me about an omelet is its simplicity. With nothing but eggs, salt, and pepper, you can produce a dish that's delicious—and cheap! That's reason enough to keep eggs in your refrigerator. So is this: Eggs are a complete protein, with all the essential amino acids your body needs, plus riboflavin; folate; vitamins B_6, B_{12}, D, and E; iron; phosphorus; and zinc. As far as technique is concerned, the main skill you need is patience: Allow the eggs to cook until set before folding the omelet over the filling. Curry powder and tomatoes add fresh, bright flavor to this version, but feel free to put your own spin on it—omelets are a canvas for creative expression. Turn this into dinner with a Watercress, Cilantro, and Arugula Salad (page 156).

CURRY-TOMATO OMELET   MAKES 1 SERVING

2 large eggs

½ teaspoon curry powder (preferably hot)

Salt

2 teaspoons extra-virgin olive oil

5 cherry tomatoes, halved

1   Break the eggs into a medium bowl, add the curry powder and a pinch of salt, and whisk until the ingredients are well combined.

2   Heat a 9½-inch nonstick skillet over medium-low heat until a drop of water instantly sizzles and evaporates, 1 to 2 minutes. Add the oil, and swirl the pan to coat the bottom. Pour in the egg mixture, covering the bottom of the pan. Let the eggs cook until they begin to set, about 2 minutes.

3   Scatter the tomato halves over one half of the omelet and cook until their juices begin to release, 1 to 3 minutes more. Slide a wide metal spatula under the empty half of the omelet and fold it onto the tomatoes, making a half-moon shape. Slide the omelet onto a plate and serve.

BISCUITS AND SCONES are my everything, so I thought morphing the two would be delicious—and it is, especially with Quince Compote. If you don't have a biscuit cutter, use a glass with a diameter of 2½ to 3 inches and a fairly thin edge.

GINGER BISCUIT-SCONES WITH QUINCE COMPOTE   MAKES 3 SMALL BISCUIT-SCONES

⅓ cup plus 1 tablespoon all-purpose flour, plus more for dusting

¼ teaspoon baking powder

¼ teaspoon baking soda

Salt

½ teaspoon light brown sugar

2 tablespoons plus 1 teaspoon chopped candied ginger

2 tablespoons cold butter, cut into cubes

2 tablespoons buttermilk

Quince Compote, for serving (recipe follows)

1   Preheat the oven to 400°F. Line a baking sheet with parchment paper.

2   Measure the ⅓ cup plus 1 tablespoon flour, the baking powder, baking soda, a pinch of salt, the sugar, candied ginger, and butter into a medium bowl. Use your hands to mix the ingredients until they form pieces about the size of peas and grapes.

3   Add the buttermilk and stir with a rubber spatula just until the ingredients are combined. (Do not overmix or aim to make a homogenous dough; it will toughen your biscuits.)

4   Generously dust a clean work surface with flour and place the dough on it. Working quickly, knead the dough into a ball, press the ball flat, and fold it over onto itself. Pat it into a 1½-inch thickness. Using a 2½- or 3-inch cutter, cut 2 biscuits from the dough. Place them on the prepared baking sheet along with any leftover dough (just form it into a round shape).

5   Place the pan in the oven and bake the biscuits for 10 to 12 minutes, until risen and golden brown. Serve warm with the compote.

. . . continued

QUINCE COMPOTE MAKES 2 CUPS

When I was a *stagaire* (intern) at the famous Parisian restaurant Taillevent, I loved to flirt with Benjamin, the garde-manger. He was not only handsome, but also made an exquisite quince compote to serve with the roasted pheasant. Before each service, I'd ask him to save me some, and soon he was sending vacuum-sealed bags of it home with me at night. This is my version of Benjamin's confection. Serve it with the Ginger Biscuit-Scones, or on yogurt (or with pheasant, of course!). Quinces are in season from October to December and look like a cross between an apple and a pear. They smell divine when ripe.

3 ripe quinces

1 cup water

1 tablespoon light brown sugar

1 teaspoon ground cinnamon

1   Peel, core, and dice the quinces. Put into a small saucepan with the water and brown sugar.

2   Set the pan over high heat and bring the mixture just to a boil. Adjust the heat to maintain a low simmer and cook, uncovered, until the fruit breaks down and the mixture thickens, 15 to 18 minutes.

3   Remove the pan from the heat and stir the cinnamon into the compote. Serve warm, or refrigerate in an airtight container. The compote can be served cold in yogurt or on toast and keeps for approximately 3 days.

A FEW SUMMERS AGO, my good friend Seiko came to visit from Paris, and was a much better guest than I was a host. Every night she cooked for me—and sometimes for my friends. Her first morning in New York, she made this fruit salad. Cutting the citrus sections from their membranes—the French call these *suprêmes*—makes for a beautiful salad. So do goji berries, which look like bright red raisins and are rich in vitamins A and C, plus fiber and a surprising amount of protein.

GOJI BERRY FRUIT SALAD MAKES 1 SERVING

1 grapefruit

1 apple

6 fresh strawberries

¼ cup fresh blueberries

2 tablespoons dried goji berries

1 Cut the grapefruit into sections or *suprêmes:* Using a sharp knife, peel away the skin and as much of the white pith as possible. Then cut toward the grapefruit's center on both sides of each membrane, cutting as close as possible. You should end up with segments of smooth flesh. Discard the membrane and put the grapefruit in a medium bowl.

2 Slice the apple and strawberries thinly. Add them to the grapefruit, along with the blueberries and goji berries. Toss gently to combine, and enjoy.

BROILING, GRILLING, OR STEWING fruit brings out its sweetness. In this recipe, sugar and cardamom caramelize on top of the grapefruit, adding a sweet, aromatic complement to its natural acidity. Enjoy this in winter when Florida and California citrus are in season.

BROILED GRAPEFRUIT WITH CARDAMOM

MAKES 1 SERVING

1 grapefruit

1 teaspoon sugar

½ teaspoon ground cardamom

1 Preheat the broiler.

2 Cut the grapefruit in half. Cover and refrigerate one half for another day. Place the other half on a cutting board and use a small serrated knife or paring knife to cut around each segment of flesh, freeing it from the membrane. Place it, cut side up, on a baking sheet.

3 In a small bowl, mix the sugar and cardamom and sprinkle it on the grapefruit.

4 Put the fruit in the oven, about 4 inches from the broiler. Broil for 2 to 3 minutes, until the grapefruit is slightly caramelized on top. Transfer to a bowl, and enjoy.

WHEN I WAKE UP HUNGRY but need to get out of the house in a hurry, this is my fast breakfast. My mom got our family into fruit smoothies in the 1990s. "You need your antioxidants, and blueberries are a good way to get them in first thing," she'd say. My parents like bananas in their smoothies. I don't, so mine is all berries. Protein powder is a must or you'll end up hungry in ten minutes. Frozen fruit makes the smoothie thick and, of course, icy cold. Handmade Almond Milk (page 38) is great in this, but store-bought milk—even regular moo juice—is fine.

DOUBLE-BERRY SMOOTHIE   MAKES 1 SERVING

1 cup almond milk

1 cup frozen blueberries

½ cup frozen whole strawberries

2 teaspoons maple syrup or honey

1 scoop protein powder

1   Put all the ingredients into a blender and process on high speed until smooth. Taste and add more sweetener if needed. Transfer to a glass, and enjoy.

BEFORE YOU ROLL YOUR EYES, let me explain. A while back, I was feeling run-down with a bad cold, and decided to go off sugar and alcohol for thirty days. I eliminated my daily cookie and glass of wine, and added green juice, usually from my favorite raw vegan shop, One Lucky Duck, on East 17th Street. It was an amazing month. I felt wildly energetic, and friends told me I had a glow. I've gone back to cookies and wine, but I've stuck with green juice, usually homemade. You won't need a pricey juicer to make it; a good blender is fine. You will need a 16-ounce glass for serving.

EMERALD ELIXIR (GOING GREEN IN THE A.M.) MAKES 1 SERVING

1 cup packed chopped Swiss chard (preferably rainbow variety)

1 cup packed chopped fresh cilantro

1 cup chopped fresh pineapple

½ cup packed chopped fresh spinach

⅓ cup coconut water

1 teaspoon honey

Juice of 1 lime

Ice cubes (optional)

1 Combine the chard, cilantro, pineapple, spinach, coconut water, honey, and lime juice in a blender. Pulse to combine and then turn the blender to its highest setting to liquefy. (You may need to stop the blender a time or two, stir the ingredients with a wooden spoon, and pulse again.) Pour into a tall glass, adding ice cubes if you prefer your juice chilled. Enjoy immediately.

A WHILE AGO, I learned about carrageenan, a seaweed derivative that's used as a thickener and stabilizer in a lot of non-lactose milks. Apparently, it can irritate your gut, so I started making my own almond milk. It's super easy, and it makes you feel like a productive member of a hippie commune. You could replace the almonds with raw, shelled, unsalted pistachios to make pistachio milk. Either way, you'll need cheesecloth, which is sold at supermarkets and kitchen supply stores. Keep the milk, tightly covered, in the refrigerator, and use it within 3 days.

HANDMADE ALMOND MILK (OR HOW TO BE A HIPPIE)

MAKES ABOUT 2 CUPS

1 cup raw unsalted almonds

4 cups water (preferably filtered)

1 Put the almonds in a medium bowl and cover with 2 cups of the water. Refrigerate, covered, at least overnight and up to 2 days.

2 Drain the almonds in a colander, rinsing them with cold running water. Transfer the nuts to a blender and add the remaining 2 cups water.

3 Pulse the blender a few times to crush the almonds. Then turn it on top speed and let it run until the mixture is smooth, 2 to 3 minutes.

4 Line a large strainer with cheesecloth and set it over a bowl large enough to hold the liquid with room to spare. Pour the almond mixture into the lined strainer and let it drip into the bowl. Once most of the milk has strained through, gather the cheesecloth into a ball and squeeze out the rest of the liquid over the strainer.

5 Transfer the milk to an airtight container (I use a mason jar) and refrigerate.

TAKE
A LUNCH

"Manhattan is a narrow island off the coast of New Jersey devoted to the pursuit of lunch."

—Raymond Sokolov

In too many offices, lunchtime is announced by the boxed smell of Stouffer's lasagna or Lean Cuisine peanut noodles wafting from the microwave. Imagine, instead, setting a place for yourself in the break room and sitting down to a Tahitian noodle sandwich with torn cilantro, shredded carrots, and sriracha or a bread salad packed with Mediterranean flavors. You would be refueling for the afternoon and enjoying an aesthetic treat at the same time. Your mood would go up a notch, and you'd be the envy of your coworkers.

Go on, live a little. Make your own lunch. You can take it one step further by bringing your own linen napkin and real silverware. Many of the recipes in this chapter, including the aforementioned noodle sandwich (page 45) and Panzanella per Una (page 64), are perfect for packing. Others, like Grilled Blue Cheese with Curried Red Onions (page 42) and Poached Egg with Frisée and Arugula Salad (page 54), are meant for pampering yourself at home. And a few, like Spinach-Feta Quiche (page 49) and Cozy Lentil Stew with Six Vegetables (page 63), make multiple servings so you can cook once and eat through the week.

A GRILLED CHEESE SANDWICH is the bear hug of comfort foods. It's difficult to screw up; a well-trained eight-year-old can make one. If you're feeling lazy, it can be dinner. When you're hung over, it seems to soak up the alcohol. Plus, you can easily add a personal touch. My version features blue cheese (my favorite is Bleu d'Auvergne), red onions, and curry. It's best on slices of a round country loaf such as pain Poilâne, but any sturdy multigrain bread is fine. I use a cast-iron skillet and extra-virgin olive oil to make the magic happen. This is great with the Watercress, Cilantro, and Arugula Salad (page 156).

GRILLED BLUE CHEESE WITH CURRIED RED ONIONS   MAKES 1 SERVING

3 teaspoons extra-virgin olive oil

½ cup sliced red onion

Salt

Freshly ground black pepper

½ teaspoon curry powder (preferably hot)

2 slices multigrain bread

1½ ounces blue cheese, crumbled

1   Heat 2 teaspoons of the olive oil in a 10-inch cast-iron skillet over medium heat, tilting the pan to coat the bottom. Add the onion, a pinch of salt, and a grind of pepper. Cook, stirring occasionally, until the onion is translucent, about 5 minutes. Stir in the curry powder and cook for another 3 minutes.

2   Using a wide metal spatula, push the onions to one side of the skillet. Add the remaining 1 teaspoon olive oil, spreading it with the spatula to coat. Put 1 slice of the bread in the skillet, let it toast until lightly browned, about 2 minutes, and flip it over. Spoon the onions onto the toasted side, spreading them to cover the surface, and arrange the cheese on top in a single layer.

3   Add the second slice of bread to the pan and let it toast until lightly browned. Place it on the first slice, toasted side down. Flip the sandwich and cook it until the second side browns and the cheese melts a bit more, about 2 minutes. Cut the sandwich in half, if desired, and serve immediately.

(when you need a hug)

WHEN I WAS TWENTY-FOUR, I had the amazing good fortune to spend four months in Tahiti working for the American Friends Service Committee. My mission was to study the effects of nuclear testing—heavy stuff—and support the development of microenterprises that sold traditional Polynesian products like vanilla beans. I lived with my boss and his beautiful young family in a tropical bungalow in the village of Faaone, tucked between a small mountain and the ocean. On lunch breaks, I sometimes went fishing or climbed the neighboring hills, picking rambutans and pomelos along the way. Some weeks I shuttled to the neighboring island of Moorea, where I worked on ecotourism projects. One weekend in Moorea, at a soccer-game concession stand, I tried the most bizarrely delicious concoction: a baguette stuffed with marinated noodles, cilantro, shredded carrots, and mushrooms, all topped with a spicy red sauce—a sort of vegetarian take on a Vietnamese banh mi. This is my version of that sandwich. Take a bite, and pretend you're in the South Pacific. The Thai hot sauce sriracha has become a supermarket staple, so you should have no trouble finding it.

TAHITIAN NOODLE SANDWICH

MAKES 1 SERVING

6 cups water

½ cup dried sliced shiitake mushrooms

Salt

1 ounce spaghetti

1 tablespoon soy sauce

1 tablespoon toasted sesame oil

1 tablespoon finely chopped fresh cilantro

1 teaspoon minced fresh ginger

1 garlic clove, minced

¼ teaspoon maple syrup

½ baguette

1 small carrot

Sriracha, for serving

1 Preheat the oven to 350°F. (If you have a toaster oven, use it instead.) In a saucepan, bring 3 cups of the water to a boil over high heat. Add the shiitake mushrooms, turn off the heat, cover the pan, and set aside until the mushrooms soften, about 25 minutes.

2 In another saucepan, bring the remaining 3 cups water to a boil over high heat. Add a couple of pinches of salt to the water, along with the pasta. Cook the spaghetti until al dente, 6 to 8 minutes.

3 Meanwhile, put the soy sauce, sesame oil, cilantro, ginger, garlic, and maple syrup in a medium bowl, and whisk to combine. Drain the noodles well and add them to the bowl. Use tongs to toss the pasta, coating it with the sauce.

4 When the shiitakes are rehydrated, drain them in a strainer, pressing out all the liquid. (Save it to add to a soup broth.) Add the mushrooms to the pasta mixture and toss.

5 Place the baguette in the oven until warmed through and lightly toasted, 3 to 4 minutes.

6 Meanwhile, peel the carrot, discarding the skin, and use the peeler to shave the flesh onto the noodles.

7 Cut the baguette in half lengthwise and fill it with the noodle mixture. Sprinkle the filling with sriracha, close the sandwich, and enjoy.

"**ALL OF HUMANKIND HAS** one thing in common: the sandwich," Liz Lemon once said on *30 Rock*. "I believe that all anyone really wants in this life is to sit in peace and eat a sandwich." I was so taken with the notion that I named this delicious sandwich in honor of Tina Fey, the NBC sitcom's creator and star. I like it on rye, but that's negotiable. This sandwich is part of my Four Meals in One medley (page 92), or it can be made with meat from a super-market rotisserie chicken. The recipe makes about 1 cup of chutney, which can be used as a spread on toast or other sandwiches. Refrigerate it for up to a week in a mason jar or other covered container or freeze it in an airtight container for up to 2 months.

ROASTED CHICKEN WITH MANGO CHUTNEY ON RYE (THE TINA FEY)

MAKES 1 SERVING

FOR THE CHUTNEY:

2 teaspoons extra-virgin olive oil

2 tablespoons chopped red onion

1 cup chopped ripe mango

1 tablespoon apple cider vinegar

1 teaspoon light brown sugar

¼ teaspoon seeded and minced
Thai chile

¼ teaspoon curry powder

Salt

1 teaspoon chopped fresh cilantro
(optional)

FOR THE SANDWICH:

2 slices rye bread

4 thick slices roasted chicken

2 lettuce leaves

1   FOR THE CHUTNEY: Heat the olive oil in a small saucepan over medium heat, tilting the pan to coat the bottom. Add the onion and cook, stirring occasionally, until translucent, about 5 minutes. Add the mango, vinegar, brown sugar, chile, curry powder, and pinch of salt. Simmer over low heat, stirring occasionally, until the mango is slightly mushy, 6 to 8 minutes. Taste and adjust the seasoning, if desired. Remove the chutney from the heat, and stir in the cilantro, if desired.

2   FOR THE SANDWICH: Toast the bread. Spread a tablespoon of mango chutney on each slice. Top it with the chicken and lettuce, close the sandwich, and enjoy.

I DON'T GENERALLY LIKE to keep a lot of leftovers in the fridge, but this is fun to have around for a few days as a ready-made lunch, snack, or dinner. I call it a quiche, but it's not your typical, ultra-creamy dairy affair. The key here is to buy frozen chopped spinach. For some reason, whole leaf spinach makes the quiche less attractive, and I'm convinced the flavors don't carry as well, either. If you forget to thaw the spinach, you can place it in a strainer over the sink, pour hot water over it, and squeeze out the moisture. There's no need to thaw the pie shell before baking.

SPINACH-FETA QUICHE (PERFECT PACKED LUNCH)

1 pound frozen chopped spinach, thawed in the refrigerator

¾ cup cubed feta cheese (about 3 ounces)

½ cup crème fraîche or full-fat sour cream

2 large eggs, beaten

1 tablespoon finely chopped oil-packed sun-dried tomatoes

¼ teaspoon salt

Freshly ground black pepper

1 (9-inch) frozen pie shell

½ cup freshly grated Parmesan cheese

1 Preheat the oven to 375°F.

2 Pour the thawed spinach into a large strainer placed over a big bowl and squeeze out as much liquid as possible. Discard the liquid (or save it to add to a soup broth), wipe out the bowl, and put the spinach in it.

3 Add the feta, crème fraîche, eggs, tomatoes, salt, and a grind of pepper to the bowl. Stir to combine the ingredients well and pour the mixture into the pie shell.

4 Put the quiche in the oven and bake for 40 minutes. Remove it from the oven and sprinkle it with the Parmesan. Return it to the oven and bake for another 10 to 12 minutes, until the cheese is melted, the quiche is firm to the touch, and the crust is golden.

5 Cool the quiche on a rack, and cut it into wedges. Serve at room temperature. Leftovers will keep, wrapped tightly in plastic wrap, in the refrigerator for up to 4 days. The quiche can also be frozen for up to 2 months. There is no need to thaw it; simply unwrap the frozen quiche, place it on a baking sheet, and put it in an oven preheated to 350°F for 30 minutes, or until warmed through.

YOU SHOULD ALWAYS HAVE at least one avocado in your fridge. They're a must for guacamole, of course, but they're also great in salads. I even add them to smoothies. *Tartine* is the French word for an open-face sandwich, and this super-simple version makes a delicious mini lunch and a perfect partner for soup. A slice of artisanal sourdough is ideal here, but any good bread will do. For a filling side, I recommend the Curry-Carrot Soup (page 121).

GUACAMOLE TARTINE   MAKES 1 SERVING

1 ripe avocado, pitted, peeled, and chopped

1 garlic clove, minced

2 teaspoons freshly squeezed lemon juice

Salt

2 slices bread

1   In a medium bowl, use a fork to mash the avocado with the garlic, lemon juice, and a pinch of salt.

2   Toast the bread.

3   Spread the mixture onto the toast, cut the slices in half, and enjoy.

I USED TO DO LIVE translation for a class at Le Cordon Bleu called Chef's Secrets, in which a French-speaking chef would teach students how to cook a simple three-course meal. I snagged this salad from one of those menus, and I love to serve it as a sophisticated lunch. Have this with a glass of cold Sancerre, and pretend you're in Paris. If your gourmet grocery store doesn't carry smoked duck breast, order it online from dartagnan.com—it's a delicious splurge. You'll have extra vinaigrette, which keeps well in the fridge and is great over steamed vegetables and fish as well as salads.

SMOKED DUCK BREAST SALAD

MAKES 1 SERVING

FOR THE SALAD:

2 teaspoons extra-virgin olive oil

5 thin slices smoked duck breast

2 small red potatoes

3 cups water

Salt

10 to 12 French green beans

4 cups mixed greens

FOR THE VINAIGRETTE:

½ cup extra-virgin olive oil

¼ cup balsamic vinegar

1 garlic clove, minced

¼ teaspoon chipotle chile powder

¼ teaspoon salt

¼ teaspoon freshly ground black pepper

1 FOR THE SALAD: Heat the oil in a 10-inch cast-iron skillet over medium-high heat, tilting the pan to coat the bottom. Cook the duck breast slices until slightly browned but still tender, 3 to 4 minutes on each side. Transfer to a plate and set aside.

2 Meanwhile, put the potatoes, water, and a few pinches of salt in a small saucepan, and bring to a boil over high heat. Adjust the heat and cook the potatoes at a brisk simmer until tender when pierced with a fork, about 15 minutes. With a slotted spoon, transfer the potatoes to a cutting board. Bring the water back to a boil, add the green beans, and blanch until bright green, about 1 minute. Drain and set aside.

3 Arrange the greens on a serving plate and place the beans on top in a single layer. Cut the potatoes in half and place them on the greens. Arrange the duck breast slices, slightly overlapping, in a fan-like pattern in the center of the salad.

4 FOR THE VINAIGRETTE: Combine the olive oil, vinegar, garlic, chipotle powder, salt, and pepper in a small jar with a tight-fitting lid and shake until emulsified and slightly thickened. Spoon 1 to 2 tablespoons of the vinaigrette over the salad and serve. Refrigerate the extra vinaigrette for up to 1 week.

POACHED EGGS ARE so much more elegant than their stinky cousins, boiled eggs, and I show you how to make them in this recipe. I would happily eat this salad with Curry-Carrot Soup (page 121), probably with a slice of Quinoa Quick Bread with Carrots and Dill (page 180).

POACHED EGG WITH FRISÉE AND ARUGULA SALAD   MAKES 1 SERVING

FOR THE POACHED EGG:

4 cups water

1 tablespoon distilled white vinegar

1 large egg

FOR THE VINAIGRETTE:

1 tablespoon extra-virgin olive oil

2 teaspoons balsamic vinegar

½ teaspoon Dijon mustard

1 garlic clove, minced

Salt

Freshly ground black pepper

TO FINISH THE SALAD:

2 cups frisée

2 cups arugula

1   FOR THE POACHED EGG: Bring the water to a boil in a large saucepan over high heat. Add the vinegar and adjust the heat to a brisk simmer.

2   Break the egg into a small bowl and pour it into the simmering water. Poach until the white turns opaque, 3 to 4 minutes. Remove the egg with a slotted spoon, place it on a clean kitchen towel to drain, and gently push it with your finger or a spoon. If it's too soft, put it back in the simmering water for another minute. (As a general rule, 4 minutes yields a firmly poached egg, and 2 minutes yields a soft one with a liquid yolk.)

3   FOR THE VINAIGRETTE: Whisk the oil, vinegar, mustard, garlic, a pinch of salt, and a grind of pepper in a medium bowl until the ingredients emulsify and thicken slightly.

4   TO FINISH THE SALAD: Add the frisée and arugula to the bowl and use your hands to toss the salad, coating the greens with the vinaigrette. Transfer the salad to a serving plate and place the poached egg on top. Garnish with a hint of freshly ground pepper. Serve immediately.

AS MUCH AS I love butter, cheese, and chocolate, I know the importance of eating healthfully, and when I do, I make sure those good-for-me dishes taste great. A case in point is this salad made with quinoa—a "super grain" (it's technically a seed) that's high in iron, calcium, and is a good source of fiber and protein. It's also lovely in this salad for lunch at your desk or a picnic at the beach. Pack some grapes or an apple and you're good to go. Fennel and mint are the big, bright flavors that make this salad extra refreshing—perfect for a summer day. This makes enough for two meals, and it will taste even better the second day. Make sure to cook the quinoa in advance; it needs to chill in the refrigerator before you assemble the salad.

PICNIC SALAD WITH QUINOA AND VEGGIES   MAKES 2 SERVINGS

FOR THE SALAD:

½ cup quinoa

1¼ cups water

2 teaspoons extra-virgin olive oil

Salt

1   FOR THE SALAD: Put the quinoa in a fine-mesh sieve and rinse it well with cold running water. (This dissolves its bitter natural coating.) Transfer it to a small saucepan, add the water, olive oil, and a couple of pinches of salt and bring to a boil over high heat. Decrease the heat, cover the pot, and simmer until the quinoa is tender and the water is absorbed, about 25 minutes. Transfer the quinoa to a medium bowl, fluff it with a fork, and refrigerate until cool, about 1 hour.

. . . *continued*

FOR THE VINAIGRETTE:

2 tablespoons extra-virgin olive oil

1 tablespoon freshly squeezed lemon juice

½ teaspoon soy sauce

½ teaspoon apple cider vinegar

1 garlic clove, minced

⅛ teaspoon salt

FOR SERVING:

½ cup halved cherry tomatoes

⅓ cup finely chopped fennel (white part only)

2 tablespoons finely chopped fresh mint

2 tablespoons finely chopped fresh flat-leaf parsley

2   FOR THE VINAIGRETTE: In another medium bowl, combine the olive oil, lemon juice, soy sauce, vinegar, garlic, and salt and whisk until emulsified and slightly thickened.

3   TO SERVE: Add the cooled quinoa to the vinaigrette along with the tomatoes, fennel, mint, and parsley. Stir well with a rubber spatula to combine. Serve at room temperature.

SMOKED FISH IS ONE of my favorite ingredients, both because I love the taste and because it's already prepared. In other words, all you have to do is open the package. Sometimes I eat smoked bluefish or mackerel with crackers and call it a meal (it's my secret singleton dinner), but serving it with a salad makes it a proper, elegant, grown-up lunch. My favorite brand of smoked mackerel, Ducktrap, is sold in supermarkets and online (gourmet-food.com is one source). As with most smoked fish, it's funky, and you'll want to brush your teeth and gargle before speaking with other humans face-to-face after eating this. Have the salad with a few slices of Quinoa Quick Bread with Carrots and Dill (page 180) or your favorite store-bought bread, toasted.

SMOKED MACKEREL SALAD WITH AVOCADO   MAKES 1 SERVING

Juice of 1 lemon

2 tablespoons extra-virgin olive oil

1 garlic clove, minced

Salt

4 cups mixed salad greens

1 ripe avocado, pitted, peeled, and sliced

1 (3½- to 4-ounce) smoked mackerel fillet

1 In a small jar with a tight-fitting lid, combine the lemon juice, olive oil, garlic, and a pinch of salt and shake until the dressing is emulsified, about 1 minute.

2 Spread the greens on a serving plate, arrange the avocado slices on top, and place the smoked mackerel on the avocado. Drizzle the salad with the dressing and serve.

I'D FORGOTTEN TO GROCERY SHOP, and when I opened the refrigerator at dinnertime, the shelves were almost bare. With kale, rice, and a few other staples, I put together this tasty meal in a bowl. The moral of the story is that you can often create something out of almost nothing. Use this recipe as a guide when you're feeling inventive and have only a few random bits in the fridge. If you have leftover rice—brown or white—you can use a cup of it here rather than cook the rice from scratch. For a hint of protein, I top this dish off with an egg—either poached or sunny-side up.

SCAVENGER HUNT FRIED RICE WITH KALE MAKES 1 SERVING

1 In a small saucepan, combine ¾ cup of the water, the rice, and 1 teaspoon of the grape seed oil. Bring to a boil over high heat, decrease the heat to low, cover the pot, and simmer the rice for 35 to 40 minutes. Let it stand, covered, off the heat, for 5 to 10 minutes.

. . . continued

4¾ cups water

⅓ cup brown rice

2 teaspoons grape seed oil

½ cup sliced red onion

Salt

2 cups chopped kale (thick ribs discarded)

1 tablespoon chopped oil-packed sun-dried tomatoes

1 garlic clove, minced

1 teaspoon toasted sesame oil

1 tablespoon distilled white vinegar

1 large egg

1½ teaspoons soy sauce

Sriracha, for serving (optional)

2　While the rice cooks, heat the remaining 1 teaspoon grape seed oil in a cast-iron skillet over medium heat, tilting the pan to coat the bottom. Put the remaining 4 cups water on to boil in a large saucepan over high heat.

3　Add the onion to the skillet and cook until translucent, about 5 minutes. Stir in a pinch of salt, the kale, tomatoes, and garlic. Cook until the kale wilts, 3 to 4 minutes. Stir in the cooked rice and sesame oil. Cover the skillet and turn off the heat.

4　Lower the heat under the water to maintain a simmer and add the vinegar. Break the egg into a small bowl and slip it into the water. Poach until the white is opaque and the yolk yields slightly to gentle pressure, 3 to 4 minutes.

5　While the egg is cooking, transfer the rice mixture to a bowl and drizzle it with the soy sauce. Remove the poached egg from the pan with a slotted spoon, let any water drain away, and place the egg on top of the rice. Season to taste with sriracha, if desired, and serve.

EVERYONE NEEDS A FEW CHEAP, healthy, go-to recipes in their back pocket, and this is one of mine. I load this stew up with vegetables and either pretend to be vegan or top it with Parmesan cheese and maybe a poached egg. If I eat it for a week, I feel kind of svelte and very virtuous. This makes enough for several meals and will keep, tightly covered, for up to 4 days in the refrigerator or 2 months in the freezer. Serve it with a green salad.

COZY LENTIL STEW WITH SIX VEGETABLES   MAKES 4 SERVINGS

2 tablespoons extra-virgin olive oil

½ cup chopped onion

1 teaspoon curry powder (preferably hot)

1 carrot, peeled and thinly sliced

2 dry-packed sun-dried tomatoes, thinly sliced

2 cups vegetable or chicken stock

1 cup water

1 cup French green Le Puy lentils or brown lentils, rinsed and drained

½ cup cubed sweet potato (½-inch cubes)

⅓ cup chopped eggplant

½ teaspoon salt

1 medium zucchini, cut into ½-inch cubes

Freshly grated Parmesan cheese (optional)

1   In a large pot (at least 2 quarts), heat the oil over medium heat, tilting the pan to coat the bottom. Add the onion and cook, stirring occasionally, until softened and translucent, about 5 minutes. Stir in the curry powder and let it cook until fragrant, about 30 seconds. Stir in the carrot and tomatoes and let them cook for a few minutes.

2   Add the stock, water, lentils, sweet potato, eggplant, and salt. Bring the mixture to a boil over high heat, and immediately decrease it to a simmer. Cook, covered, stirring occasionally, until the lentils and vegetables are tender and the stew thickens, about 45 minutes. Add a little water if it gets too dry.

3   Stir in the zucchini and cook until tender, about 10 minutes. Serve the stew in a soup bowl and top it with Parmesan, if desired.

THIS JUST MIGHT BE my favorite salad. Because there's no lettuce, it can be made up to a few hours ahead. It's also fast, filling, and Italian, so it checks a lot of my boxes. Originally from Tuscany, this salad is ideal for leftover bread and juicy tomatoes. Some people add basil, which is delicious, but I use dried oregano. I also add feta and Greek olives, making this a pan-Mediterranean panzanella. On a hot summer day, it's a meal in itself.

PANZANELLA PER UNA   MAKES 1 SERVING

2 tablespoons extra-virgin olive oil

2½ teaspoons balsamic vinegar

1 garlic clove, minced

½ teaspoon dried oregano

Salt

1 cucumber, peeled and chopped

1 cup cubed stale bread (from a rustic country loaf or baguette)

1 cup chopped tomato

4 ounces feta cheese, crumbled

¼ cup chopped red onion

6 Kalamata olives, pitted and chopped

1   In a large bowl, combine the olive oil, vinegar, garlic, oregano, and a pinch of salt. Whisk until emulsified. Add the cucumber, bread, tomato, feta, onion, and olives. Use your hands to toss the salad and evenly distribute the ingredients. Serve at room temperature.

MEALS WITH MEAT

"The only time to eat diet food is while you're waiting for the steak to cook."

—Julia Child

Eat less meat to help the planet, save animals, and save yourself. You know the drill. I eat meat only three or four times a month, and when I do, these are the recipes I turn to. Some, like Duck Shepherd's Pie (page 90), were inspired by fantastic restaurant meals. Others, like Mood-Boosting Rib Eye (page 77), started out as recommendations from my favorite butcher shops. Most were inventions to suit my random carnivorous cravings.

Speaking of butcher shops, allow me a soapbox moment about meat. Cooking for yourself as an act of self-care means buying high-quality ingredients, and I feel strongly about the kind of meat you should buy. If at all possible, patronize a butcher shop that specializes in pasture-raised beef, pork, lamb, and poultry. That means the animals have been outdoors for most of their lives, grazing on grass (or, in the case of chickens, pecking at bugs) as nature intended, rather than being shut inside 24-7 and subsisting on an all-grain diet. Good butchers will verify that the animals they sell are raised by farmers who don't administer unnecessary antibiotics or use genetically modified grain. (A really great butcher also sells house-made stocks—a huge convenience and often better than what you would make at home.) If there's not a butcher shop near you, most supermarkets carry free-range, pasture-raised, grass-fed, or organic meat products. Yes, it's more expensive, but you're worth it.

BEEF STEW IS FOR WINTER NIGHTS when you're in no rush to eat and want a substantial meal. This is a semi-longish recipe—about 90 minutes start to finish—but only requires about 15 minutes of prep time, and it's so worth it. I make this stew when I've got a partial bottle of red wine—enough for the pot plus a glass with dinner. It doesn't have to be a great bottle—by the time you add the stock, meat, and vegetables, even an OK wine will provide a nice backbone to hold it all together. Don't skimp on the meat, though. Go for the best you can afford, preferably pasture-raised. Complete the meal with a simple green salad and a slice of hearty bread. Unless you're famished, this will make enough for two meals, which is great, because the stew tastes even better the second day.

RED WINE BEEF STEW FOR A COLD WINTER'S NIGHT

MAKES 1 OR 2 SERVINGS

1 tablespoon extra-virgin olive oil, plus more if needed

½ pound beef for stew (chuck), cut into 2-inch chunks

1 cup chopped onion (1 medium-large onion)

2 garlic cloves, chopped

4 cups good-quality beef stock

2 medium carrots, peeled and cut into ¼-inch rounds

1 large red or white potato, cubed

5 dry-packed sun-dried tomatoes, chopped

½ cup red wine

Salt

1   Heat the oil in a medium Dutch oven or other heavy-bottomed pot over medium-high heat, tilting the pan to coat the bottom. Add the beef and let it brown well on all sides, turning as needed, 5 to 10 minutes total. Use tongs or a wide metal spatula to transfer the beef to a plate.

2   Add the onion to the pot (along with a bit more oil if necessary) and cook, stirring often, until translucent, about 5 minutes. Add the garlic and cook, stirring, until fragrant, about 1 minute.

3   Return the beef to the pot and add the stock, carrots, potatoes, tomatoes, wine, and a couple of pinches of salt. Raise the heat to high, and when the liquid begins to boil, turn it down to maintain a gentle simmer. (If a brownish foam develops on the surface, skim it off with a spoon.) Cook the stew, covered, until the meat and vegetables are tender, about 1 hour.

4   Uncover the pot, taste to adjust seasoning, and simmer the stew until the liquid has thickened and concentrated, 10 to 15 minutes. Serve hot.

THE EXERCISE OF PREPARING SUPPER

You made it through the day. And you accomplished what you set out to do at work. Along the way you had fun conversations with your coworkers about television, books, movies, life. You had lunch and worked some more. Late in the afternoon, maybe things went fuzzy. Focus declined. There was some drama. Your boss got mad. No matter. You persevered, and finally, the sacred hour has arrived: time to leave.

You get home. What will you eat? Food may not be the first thing on your mind. Maybe you need a glass of wine or a cocktail. Was the day exhilarating? Good. You've got energy to spare. Pull out all the stops and get creative in the kitchen. Was it draining? Put in the stops. Are there any cookies in the cupboard?

A lot of what you eat for dinner comes down to two things—your energy level and what's in your larder. If you do strategic shopping and keep a pantry stocked with the basics (see page 2), you can make a good meal on the fly.

No matter what kind of day it's been, the first thing I do is change clothes. Sometimes I stretch out to review the details of the day and let them go. Then I put on music and look for a bite to sustain me while I cook. My nibbles are random—nuts, chocolate, olives. If there's a log of cookie dough in the freezer, I might cut a couple of slices to bake and eat while I figure out a meal.

Why, you may ask, don't I just order in? It happens, but honestly, the food is usually disappointing, and I know I can make something better—even if it's a simple omelet and salad. Plus, once I'm out of my work clothes and the music is on, this part of the day is dedicated to relaxing. Cooking isn't a chore—it's the way I unwind.

Music is a key ingredient. When I want to relive the 1980s, neighbors might hear Grace Jones, Culture Club, or David Bowie drifting from my apartment. If I've just come back from hip-hop dance class, cue Biggie Smalls, The Roots, or Michael Jackson. When I'm in a French state of mind, I turn to Edith Piaf and Brigitte Bardot. Neighbors with a view into my apartment may also see me dancing—suppertime is showtime in my home. So get your cooking playlist together and get going. You deserve a good meal!

CERTAIN INGREDIENTS WORK PERFECTLY together, and this recipe is a sparkling example. It's a version of a dish by Chef Christophe Pelé, formerly of La Bigarrade in Paris, that blew me away at a Le Fooding event a few years ago. Le Fooding is a French organization that creates amazing festivals to celebrate food and foster "an appetite for newness, imagination, quality, a love of beauty in the ordinary, a rejection of what is boring, and a desire to take your time with your food," as its manifesto states. The soy sauce, sesame oil, lime, and ginger hit all the right notes of salty, smoky, citrusy, and spicy. It's a quick dish, too. Like Chef Pelé, I serve it over arugula, but if you feel the need for a starch, basmati rice or couscous is the ticket. Cantaloupe cubes are nice on the side. Many markets sell meat cut and packaged for stir-fry, which is a time-saving option here. If you end up with leftovers, you can use them as a filling for Beef Tacos (page 79).

SOY-LIME BEEF STIR-FRY (LE FOODING'S BEST BITE)

MAKES 1 OR 2 SERVINGS

2 tablespoons toasted sesame oil

2 tablespoons extra-virgin olive oil

1 tablespoon soy sauce

3 garlic cloves, minced

2-inch piece fresh ginger, peeled and minced

Juice of 1 lime

3 cups arugula

Salt

½ pound flank or other beef steak (preferably pasture-raised), sliced across the grain into thin strips

Grated zest of 1 lemon

1 In a medium bowl, combine the sesame oil, 1 tablespoon of the olive oil, the soy sauce, garlic, ginger, and lime juice. Set aside. Arrange the arugula on a dinner plate and set aside.

2 Heat the remaining 1 tablespoon sesame oil in a 10-inch cast-iron skillet over medium-high heat. Sprinkle a pinch or two of salt over the beef and add it to the skillet. Cook it, stirring, until done to your liking, 2 to 4 minutes.

3 Use tongs to arrange the beef over the arugula. Sprinkle the zest over the meat. Whisk the garlic-ginger mixture until well combined and pour it over all. Serve immediately.

SOME OF THE WORST meals I've eaten have been on Valentine's Day. There was the time in Paris when a guy took me to Kentucky Fried Chicken on February 14. And there was another time that a delicious boyfriend and I picked an adorable-looking restaurant that served genuinely horrible food. Dud dates make you appreciate the pleasure of your own company, so I was surprised to find myself feeling a little down in the dumps to be single when another Valentine's Day rolled around. Fortunately, I had the good sense to buy a gorgeous steak from Fleischer's butcher shop in Brooklyn and a fabulous bottle of Montefalco Rosso (a robust red with Sangiovese, Sagrantino, Cabernet Sauvignon, and Merlot grapes) from Enoteca DiPalo in Little Italy. I took them home, cooked the steak just the way the butcher recommended (see below), enjoyed a glass of wine with it, and had a blissful Valentine's Day after all.

MOOD-BOOSTING RIB EYE (OR VALENTINE'S DAY: AN UNROMANTIC COMEDY) MAKES 1 SERVING

1   Set the steak on a plate on the counter for at least 20 minutes and up to 1 hour to take the chill off (this makes for more even cooking).

. . . continued

1 (20- to 22-ounce) bone-in rib eye steak (preferably pasture-raised)

6 teaspoons grape seed oil

1 medium potato, thinly sliced

Coarse salt

Freshly ground black pepper

2 cups packed fresh baby spinach

2   Preheat the oven to 400°F.

3   Set a 10-inch cast-iron skillet over medium-high heat and add 2 teaspoons of the grape seed oil, tilting the pan to coat the bottom. Arrange the potato slices in the pan in a single layer, season lightly with salt, and cook until they begin to brown, about 2 minutes. Use a wide metal spatula to flip the potatoes and cook until tender when pierced with a fork, 2 to 3 minutes more. Remove the pan from the heat.

4   While the potatoes cook, place a large cast-iron skillet over medium-high heat and add 3 teaspoons of the grape seed oil, tilting the pan to coat the bottom. Generously season the steak on both sides with salt and pepper and place it in the pan. Sear the steak for 4 minutes without moving it, then turn with tongs and sear the other side for 4 minutes without moving it. Using an oven mitt to protect your hand, transfer the skillet to the hot oven to cook for 4 minutes. Remove the skillet from the oven and use tongs to transfer the steak to a cutting board to rest.

5   Push the potatoes to one side of the skillet, add the remaining 1 teaspoon oil to the empty side, and heat over medium-high heat. Add the spinach and a pinch of salt and cook, stirring occasionally, until wilted and bright green, 3 to 5 minutes. Taste the spinach and potatoes and adjust the seasoning if desired.

6   Arrange the steak, potatoes, and spinach on serving plates and enjoy, preferably with a glass of robust red wine.

NOT LONG AGO, I saw comedian Aziz Ansari on tour. He made me laugh for two hours straight—and impressed me with his deep love of tacos, which he talked about at length. Inspired, I set about learning how to prepare all the ingredients that make a taco delicious: pico de gallo, guacamole, and, for this one, nicely sautéed beef. (If your market sells quality beef cut and packaged for stir-fry, feel free to use it here.) Tacos are great for dinner (or anytime, really) because it's like you're having a little party for yourself. Obviously, they're also fun to make for friends, and this recipe can easily be multiplied. Have these with a cold Negra Modelo beer, and raise your glass to Aziz.

BEEF TACOS (INSPIRED BY AZIZ ANSARI) MAKES 1 SERVING

FOR THE PICO DE GALLO FOR ONE:

½ cup chopped cherry tomatoes

1 tablespoon minced red onion

1 tablespoon freshly squeezed lime juice

1 tablespoon minced fresh cilantro

⅛ teaspoon seeded and minced Thai chile

Salt

1 **FOR THE PICO DE GALLO FOR:** Place the tomatoes, onion, lime juice, cilantro, and chile in a small bowl. Add a pinch of salt, taste, and adjust the seasoning, if desired. Stir to combine and set aside.

2 **FOR THE GUACAMOLE:** In another small bowl, combine the avocado, onion, lime juice, cilantro, and chile. Using a fork, mash the ingredients together. Season with salt (I suggest 2 pinches), taste and adjust the seasoning, and set aside.

3 **TO FINISH THE DISH:** Heat the oil in a small cast-iron skillet over medium-high heat, tilting the pan to coat the bottom. Add the beef, season with a pinch of salt and a grind of pepper, and cook, stirring, until done to your liking, 1 to 3 minutes.

. . . continued

FOR THE GUACAMOLE FOR ONE:

½ medium ripe avocado, chopped
(about ½ cup)

1 tablespoon minced red onion

1 tablespoon freshly squeezed
lime juice

1 tablespoon minced fresh cilantro

⅛ teaspoon seeded and minced
Thai chile

Salt

TO FINISH THE DISH:

2 teaspoons extra-virgin olive oil

¼ pound flank or other beef steak
(preferably pasture-raised), sliced
across the grain into thin strips

Salt

Freshly ground black pepper

2 or 3 (6-inch or smaller) corn
tortillas

1 lime, halved

4   Heat another cast-iron skillet over low heat, stack the tortillas in it, and warm them, turning the stack once, for about 2 minutes per side. (Or, if you have a microwave, wrap them in a damp paper towel and heat on high power for 30 seconds.)

5   To serve, spread guacamole on each tortilla. Top it with the beef and pico de gallo and finish the tacos with a squeeze of lime juice.

BURGERS: THE ULTIMATE PICK-ME-UP

A great burger brightens my day because it's got two things I love: hot, fat-flecked meat (I'm convinced fat makes people happy) and bread. That combination plus tasty condiments is my personal, deeply satisfying antidote to grouchy moods. Like a grilled cheese sandwich, a hamburger is a canvas for your imagination. I like to keep it simple with ground beef (an 80-20 ratio of meat to fat is ideal) and add just salt, pepper, and garlic (1 minced clove per ¼ pound), plus maybe a little blue cheese on top. As you'll see in the recipes ahead, I complement ground lamb with Kalamata olives and feta cheese and ground pork with curry powder and shredded coconut. To house the burger, I like a good brioche or challah bun. The best thing about burgers is that they're super fast to make yet completely filling. Here are a few of my favorites to get you started.

THIS HOMAGE TO ONE of my favorite places combines the three ingredients I most associate with Greece—lamb, feta, and Kalamata olives. Keep the theme going with Greek Salad (page 144) or Jalapeño-Watermelon Salad (page 155).

LAMB BURGER (AN ODE TO GREECE)

MAKES 1 SERVING

¼ pound ground lamb

6 Kalamata olives, pitted and finely chopped

1 garlic clove, minced

Salt

Freshly ground black pepper

¼ cup diced or crumbled feta cheese

2 teaspoons extra-virgin olive oil

1 burger bun

3 or 4 fresh mint leaves

Ketchup, for serving (optional)

1 Preheat the oven to 350°F. (If you have a toaster oven, use it instead.)

2 In a small bowl, combine the lamb, olives, garlic, a pinch of salt, and a grind of pepper. Mix the ingredients with your hand and form into two patties, each about ½ inch thick. Mound the feta in the middle of one patty, top it with the other patty, and pinch the edges of the meat together all around to seal in the cheese.

3 Set a cast-iron skillet over medium-high heat and add the olive oil, tilting the pan to coat the bottom. Add the meat patty and cook, turning once, until nicely browned, 4 to 6 minutes per side.

4 Meanwhile, split the bun and place it in the oven for 3 to 4 minutes to brown.

5 Layer the mint leaves on the bottom half of the bun, place the burger on top, spread with ketchup, if desired, close the bun, and enjoy.

DICKSON'S FARMSTAND MEATS at Chelsea Market sells amazing premade, super-thick patties that are studded with bacon, making them deliciously juicy. The minced bacon cooks along with the beef, adding a smoky note. Here's my homemade version, which is great with Mason Jar Red Cabbage Salad (page 140).

HAPPINESS IS A BACON BURGER

MAKES 1 SERVING

¼ pound 80% lean ground beef (preferably pasture-raised)

2 bacon strips, finely chopped

Salt

Freshly ground black pepper

Extra-virgin olive oil

1 burger bun

Ketchup, for serving

2 lettuce leaves (optional)

1 thinly sliced red onion (optional)

1 Preheat the oven to 350°F. (If you have a toaster oven, use it instead.)

2 In a medium bowl, use your hands to combine the ground beef with the bacon, seasoning the mixture with 2 pinches of salt and a grind of black pepper. Form the meat into a patty that's about 1 inch thick.

3 Set a cast-iron skillet over medium-high heat and add the olive oil, tilting the pan to coat the bottom. Add the meat patty and cook, turning once, until nicely browned but still juicy, 4 to 6 minutes per side.

4 Meanwhile, split the bun and place it in the oven for 3 to 4 minutes to brown.

5 Spread ketchup on both halves of the bun, place the burger on the bottom bun, arrange the lettuce and sliced onion, if desired, on top, close the bun, and serve immediately.

I CREATED THIS RECIPE when the carnivore counter at my Whole Foods Market was out of every other kind of ground meat. Sweet coconut and hot curry do wonders for the mild meat. To Be Eaten Only in Season Tomato Salad (page 138) goes well on the side.

SPICY PORK BURGER WITH COCONUT

MAKES 1 SERVING

¼ pound ground pork

1 tablespoon unsweetened shredded coconut

1 garlic clove, minced

¼ teaspoon hot curry powder

Salt

2 teaspoons extra-virgin olive oil

1 burger bun

Sriracha, for serving

¼ cup fresh baby spinach leaves

4 thin slices ripe avocado (optional)

1 Preheat the oven to 350°F. (If you have a toaster oven, use it instead.)

2 In a medium bowl, combine the pork, coconut, garlic, curry powder, and a pinch of salt. Use your hands to mix the ingredients and shape them into a patty that's about 1 inch thick.

3 Set a cast-iron skillet over medium-high heat and add the olive oil, tilting the pan to coat the bottom. Add the meat patty and cook, turning once, until nicely browned but still juicy, 4 to 6 minutes per side.

4 Meanwhile, split the bun and place it in the oven for 3 to 4 minutes to toast.

5 Spread sriracha on both halves of the bun, arrange the baby spinach and avocado, if desired, on the bottom, top it with the burger, close the bun, and serve immediately.

THERE ARE TWO REASONS why I'm not a vegetarian: bacon and lamb. Lamb chops are the fastest and most deliciously meaty meal I know. You can be bold with seasoning (think curry) or keep it simple. In this recipe, I go classic with garlic and rosemary, placed on the bottom of the pan. By the time the lamb is done, they're too charred to eat, but the meat retains their flavor. I suggest you serve these chops alongside Curry Sautéed Kale (page 136) or Curry-Carrot Soup (page 121).

LAMB I LOVE YOU: CHOPS

MAKES 1 SERVING

4 lamb chops (about ½ pound total)

Salt

Freshly ground black pepper

2 teaspoons extra-virgin olive oil

1 teaspoon finely chopped fresh rosemary

1 garlic clove, minced

2 fresh rosemary sprigs

1 Lightly season both sides of each chop with salt and pepper.

2 Heat the oil in a 10-inch cast-iron skillet over medium-high heat, tilting the pan to coat the bottom. Spread the chopped rosemary, rosemary sprigs, and garlic in the pan and place the lamb chops on top in a single layer.

3 Cook the lamb, turning once, until the exterior is browned and a bit crisp and the interior is cooked to your liking (about 3 minutes per side for medium-rare, and 4 to 5 minutes for medium-well, my preference). Serve immediately.

I NEVER KNEW HOW MUCH I could love duck and potatoes until I ate *parmentier de canard confit* at a hotel called Mama Shelter in Paris. The duck was tender, the potatoes were hearty, and I was hooked. This has become my go-to cold-weather meal when I'm feeling fancy. A *parmentier* is a rustic casserole of meat and potatoes, not unlike a shepherd's pie. Duck confit, which is salt-cured and then poached in its own fat, is what makes this dish special. It's sold, vacuum-packed, in many gourmet shops. If you can't find it locally, purchase it online from D'Artagnan (dartagnan.com). This is a great dish for a dinner party. Just multiply the ingredients by the number of guests and cook as directed in individual ramekins. Complete the meal with Fennel, Arugula, and Orange Zest Salad (page 141).

DUCK SHEPHERD'S PIE (PARMENTIER DE CANARD CONFIT)

MAKES 1 SERVING

1 large russet potato
(about 9 ounces)

Salt

1 confit duck leg (about 5 ounces)

1 teaspoon extra-virgin olive oil

½ cup diced onion

1 shallot, minced

Freshly ground black pepper

¼ cup whole milk

1 tablespoon crème fraîche

Pinch of ground nutmeg

1 Preheat the oven to 400°F.

2 Peel the potato, cut it into chunks, and add it to a saucepan with water to cover and a pinch of salt. Bring it to a boil over high heat, decrease the heat to maintain a brisk simmer, and cook the potato until tender when pierced with a fork, about 15 minutes.

3 Meanwhile, remove the duck meat from the bone and chop it. (Discard the bone and any fatty skin.)

4 Heat the oil in a 10-inch cast-iron skillet over medium heat, tilting the pan to coat the bottom. Add the onion and shallot and cook until slightly golden brown, 3 to 5 minutes. Add the duck meat and a grind of pepper, decrease the heat to medium-low, and cook for 5 minutes, stirring occasionally. The meat should be slightly browned but still moist. Taste and add salt if needed. Set the pan aside off the heat.

5 Drain the potato well, transfer it to a large bowl, and mash with a fork or potato masher, adding the milk, crème fraîche, a pinch of salt, a grind of pepper, and the nutmeg. When the mixture is fluffy, taste and adjust the seasoning, if desired.

6 Spread half the duck mixture on the bottom of a 4-inch ramekin. Mix half the mashed potato into the remaining duck and spread it over the meat in the ramekin. Spread the remaining mashed potato over all and smooth the top with the back of a fork.

7 Place the ramekin on a baking sheet, set it in the oven, and bake for about 20 minutes, or until the top layer of mashed potatoes is slightly browned. Remove it from the oven and let it cool for a few minutes before serving.

ROASTING A CHICKEN USED to be an intimidating concept to me. The bird seemed big, it couldn't be cooked on the stovetop, and in my mind only a mom, grandma, or some other official adult had the necessary expertise. Then I was commissioned to test a group of recipes, and roasted chicken was on the list. It turns out it isn't difficult at all. Now I think everyone should know how to roast a chicken, if only to enjoy the head start it gives you on nearly a week's worth of meals: tacos on Tuesday (sub 1 cup chopped chicken meat for the beef on page 79), chicken salad on Wednesday (mix 1 cup chopped chicken with baby spinach, cherry tomatoes, and vinaigrette), and a Tina Fey sandwich on Thursday (page 47).

What makes this recipe special is the combination of sage, rosemary, lemon, and tarragon stuffed into the bird's cavity. It smells divine while roasting, and the meat acquires a lush citrus-herb flavor. Roasted Vegetables with Tahini Vinaigrette (page 135) would be great on the side. You will need a meat thermometer to make sure the chicken is properly cooked. If yours is instant-read rather than traditional, pull the bird out of the oven after 45 minutes and check the temperature in the thickest part of the thigh, avoiding the bone.

FOUR MEALS IN ONE: TARRAGON-ROASTED CHICKEN

MAKES 4 SERVINGS

. . . continued

1 (2½- to 3-pound) whole chicken (preferably organic and free-range)

2 lemons, halved

Salt

6 sprigs fresh tarragon, coarsely torn

4 fresh sage leaves, coarsely torn

2 or 3 fresh rosemary sprigs

3 tablespoons extra-virgin olive oil

Freshly ground black pepper

1   Preheat the oven to 400°F.

2   Rinse the chicken inside and out under cold running water. Pat it dry with paper towels.

3   Set the chicken in a roasting pan and squeeze the juice of 1 lemon over it, inside and out. Generously season the chicken with salt, inside and out. Push half the remaining lemon all the way into the cavity, stuff in the tarragon, sage, and rosemary, and add the remaining lemon half, like a cap for the cavity. Drizzle the olive oil over the chicken, rubbing to coat the bird well, and grind pepper all over it.

4   Position a meat thermometer in the thickest part of the thigh, avoiding the bone. Place the roasting pan in the oven and roast the chicken for 45 to 50 minutes, until the skin is golden brown and the temperature reaches 165°F. Let it rest for about 10 minutes before carving and serving.

TARRAGON-ROASTED CHICKEN MONDAY

See opposite page

TACOS ON TUESDAY

Sub 1 cup chopped chicken meat for the beef on page 79

FOUR MEALS IN ONE:

CHICKEN SALAD WEDNESDAY

Mix 1 cup chopped chicken with baby spinach, cherry tomatoes, and vinaigrette

TINA FEY SANDWICH THURSDAY

Page 47

SEAFOOD SUPPERS

"Just as we'd seek out the brightest farmers' market peas or the tastiest free-range chicken, we'll look to our fishmonger for the best fish. We'll want it wild, fresh-caught, as local as possible; we'll try new fish, ranging beyond cod and tuna to smaller, sustainable, tasty types like sardines."

—Betsy Andrews, *Saveur* magazine

I fell in love with Tahiti on Valentine's Day 1998. I arrived that night at Fa'a'a International Airport in Papeete after flying for six hours from Honolulu. My boss, Gabi, put a gorgeous lei of orchids over my head in welcome, and we piled my luggage and ourselves into his car for the one-hour drive to Faaone. There weren't many lights, so I couldn't see much, but the soft, warm, dewy air told me this was a tropical place.

I settled into a loft-like bungalow on the grounds of the compound Gabi shared with his partner, Suzanne, and their two youngest children. It was surrounded by mape (Tahitian chestnut), coconut, rambutan, and other fruit trees, and there were flowers everywhere—heliconia, gardenias, hibiscus, orchids, jasmine. The outdoors were like a garden and an apothecary in one. When I took walks with the kids, Raru and Terahi, they seemed to know the name of every plant and how to use it. "Eat this and it sweetens anything you taste afterward," they would tell me. "Eat that when you feel sick. Put this in your hair and it will feel just like Pantene conditioner." Some nights I went shrimping with Suzanne—my education in how scavenger shellfish eat and hide. Other times we would grab nets and go fishing in the ocean; it was just across the road. I learned how to catch, kill, and clean fish, and ate more of it than I ever have in my life.

Seafood is an ideal ingredient for a solo supper. It's generally inexpensive to purchase in single portions and is quick and easy to cook. For the most basic prep, all you need is fresh lemon juice, salt, maybe some garlic, and a little olive oil. The key is starting with the freshest, most sustainable seafood. It's not as simple as walking across the road to the ocean and dropping a net in, but a knowledgeable fishmonger can guide you to good choices. So can programs like the Monterey Bay Aquarium's Seafood Watch (seafoodwatch.org), which recommends fish and shellfish to buy and avoid, and the Marine Stewardship Council (msc.org), which certifies sustainable seafood.

When it comes to freshness, fish should smell of the ocean and, when whole, have clear eyes and firm, shiny skin. Be sure to eat it within 48 hours of bringing it home. In the meantime, wrap it in parchment paper, seal it in a plastic bag, and place it in the coldest part of the refrigerator (usually the back of the top or bottom shelf). In a pinch, flash-frozen seafood is an option.

MY FAMILY AND I EAT this over Summer Vacation Sesame Noodles and Sugar Snap Peas (page 127) when we're on Martha's Vineyard—and when we're not but would like to be. It's one of the fastest, most delicious dinners ever.

PAN-SEARED TUNA (THIS IS WHAT I ATE ON HOLIDAY) MAKES 1 SERVING

Juice of 1 lime

2 tablespoons minced fresh ginger

1 garlic clove, minced

⅛ teaspoon salt

⅛ teaspoon freshly ground black pepper

¼ pound sushi-grade tuna, skin removed

1 tablespoon extra-virgin olive oil

1   Combine the lime juice, ginger, garlic, salt, and pepper in a shallow dish. Add the tuna and set it aside to marinate for 5 to 10 minutes, turning the fish halfway through.

2   Heat the olive oil in a 10-inch cast-iron skillet over medium-high heat for 1 minute, tilting the pan to coat the bottom. Remove the tuna from the marinade, shaking off the liquid, and place the fish in the pan. Allow it to sear, without disturbing it, for about 2 minutes. Pour the remaining marinade over the tuna. Turn the fish over and sear the second side for 1 to 2 minutes. It should be deeply browned outside but still pink in the middle. (Cut into it to check.)

3   Remove the tuna from the pan. Serve immediately.

I WAS INTRODUCED TO SHISO, an Asian member of the mint family, at Cha An, a Japanese teahouse I love in New York's East Village. It has an almost smoky flavor that I thought would work well with salmon. It does—and is even better combined with toasted sesame oil and maple syrup. Look for shiso or its Korean cousin, perilla, at Asian markets. I like to serve this dish with the Watercress, Cilantro, and Arugula Salad (page 156). Save half the fish for Second-Day Salmon with Linguine (page 113).

ROASTED SALMON WITH SHISO AND SESAME MAPLE SYRUP

MAKES 2 SERVINGS

1 (½-pound) salmon fillet

1 teaspoon freshly squeezed lemon juice

Salt

½ teaspoon maple syrup

½ teaspoon soy sauce

½ teaspoon toasted sesame oil

3 fresh shiso leaves, thinly sliced

1 Preheat the oven to 375°F.

2 Place the salmon in a shallow baking pan that's just big enough to hold it. Sprinkle it with the lemon juice and a pinch of salt.

3 In a small bowl, mix the maple syrup, soy sauce, and sesame oil, and pour over the fish, using a rubber spatula to scrape out every last drop.

4 Place the pan in the oven and roast for 10 to 12 minutes, or until the fish is opaque and flakes when pierced with a knife. Remove it from the oven, sprinkle with the shiso leaves, and serve.

LESS IS MORE when it comes to mackerel—just add a pinch of salt, a healthy dose of lemon juice, and capers. Mackerel is the perfect choice for a busy pescatarian trying to do the right thing. It cooks quickly, is brimming with heart-healthy omega-3 fatty acids, and is one of the more sustainable fish. Berbere-Roasted Asparagus (page 133) are great on the side.

MACKEREL WITH LEMON AND CAPERS (KEEP IT SIMPLE) MAKES 1 SERVING

1 (¼- to ⅓-pound) mackerel fillet, skin on

½ teaspoon rinsed and chopped capers (preferably salt-packed)

½ teaspoon extra-virgin olive oil

Juice of ½ lemon

Salt

1 Preheat the oven to 375°F.

2 Place the mackerel in a shallow baking pan that's just big enough to hold it. Sprinkle it with the capers, olive oil, lemon juice, and a pinch of salt.

3 Set the pan in the oven and roast for 9 to 10 minutes, until the fish is opaque and flakes when pierced with a knife. Transfer to a plate and serve immediately.

I'M ACTUALLY A FAN of tinned sardines, but they stink up a room and give you hideously bad breath. (Sardine Etiquette 101: Eat them in private and brush your teeth afterward or, if you must eat them around others, apologize in advance.) Fresh sardines, on the other hand, smell of the ocean. Like mackerel, they're lightning fast to prepare and are good for you and sustainable. Serve Fennel, Arugula, and Orange Zest Salad (page 141) alongside.

SKILLET SARDINES (BE A MINIMALIST)   MAKES 1 SERVING

2 to 3 teaspoons extra-virgin olive oil

2 fresh sardines (2 to 3 ounces each), cleaned and scaled with heads on

Salt

Juice of 1 lemon

1   Heat the olive oil in a 10-inch cast-iron skillet over medium-high heat for 1 minute, tilting the pan to coat the bottom. Season the sardines with 2 generous pinches of salt and place them in the pan. Fry until the fish curve slightly and the eyes turn white, 3 to 4 minutes per side.

2   Transfer the sardines to a plate, douse with the lemon juice, and serve.

(be decadent)

WHY SHOULD FISH have all the fun? Make tacos with buttery lobster. It's healthy to splurge once in a while. Buy your lobster already cooked from a reputable seafood shop or supermarket.

LOBSTER TACOS   MAKES 1 SERVING

½ teaspoon butter

1 garlic clove, minced

3 to 4 ounces cooked lobster meat, cut into ½-inch slices

Salt

1 lime, halved

2 or 3 (6-inch or smaller) corn tortillas

Guacamole for One (page 80)

Pico de Gallo for One (page 79)

1 Melt the butter in a small cast-iron skillet over medium-high heat, tilting the pan to coat the bottom. Add the garlic and cook, stirring, until fragrant, 1 to 2 minutes. Add the lobster and heat, stirring to coat with the garlic butter, for 1 to 2 minutes. Sprinkle with a pinch of salt.

2 Transfer the lobster to a small bowl, squeeze the juice of half a lime over it, and set aside.

3 Heat another cast-iron skillet over low heat, stack the tortillas in it, and warm them, turning the stack once, for about 2 minutes per side. (Or wrap them in a damp paper towel and microwave on high power for 30 seconds.)

4 To serve, spread the guacamole on each tortilla. Top it with the lobster and pico de gallo and finish the tacos with a squeeze of lime juice from the remaining lime half.

SOMETIMES YOU WANT to be a baller. A shot caller. Pretend you're Sean "Puffy" Combs circa 1990 or Jay Z or Beyoncé today. Drink Champagne. Take your yacht for a spin around St. Barts. Eat lobster. Here's a recipe to make you feel like you're living the glamorous life. Buy your lobster already cooked from a reputable seafood shop or supermarket. If you end up with leftovers, indulge yourself a second night with Lobster Tacos (page 109).

LOBSTER PASTA SALAD

MAKES 1 SERVING

4 cups water

Salt

2 ounces linguine fini or cavatappi

4 teaspoons extra-virgin olive oil

1 teaspoon minced garlic

3 to 4 ounces cooked lobster meat, coarsely chopped

2 tablespoons freshly squeezed lemon juice, plus more as needed

8 cherry tomatoes, halved

6 Kalamata olives, pitted and chopped

2 tablespoons thinly sliced scallions

1 tablespoon minced fresh flat-leaf parsley

1 teaspoon minced fresh mint

½ teaspoon rinsed and chopped capers (preferably salt-packed)

1 In a large pot, bring the water and a healthy pinch of salt to a boil over high heat. Add the pasta and cook, stirring occasionally, until al dente, 6 to 8 minutes. Drain, transfer to a large bowl, and drizzle with 2 teaspoons of the olive oil.

2 While the pasta cooks, heat the remaining 2 teaspoons oil in a 10-inch cast-iron skillet over medium heat. Add the garlic and cook, stirring, until fragrant, about 1 minute. Add the lobster and heat through, 1 to 2 minutes, stirring to coat with the garlic and oil. Transfer the lobster to a small bowl and pour the lemon juice over it.

3 Add the lobster and lemon juice to the pasta, along with the tomatoes, olives, scallions, parsley, mint, and capers. Toss with tongs to combine well. Taste for seasoning and add salt and more lemon juice as needed. Serve warm.

MY FRIEND SEIKO whipped this up for dinner when she stayed at my place on vacation. It's pretty simple: leftover salmon (perhaps from Roasted Salmon with Shiso and Sesame Maple Syrup, page 104), crème fraîche (which makes an instant cream sauce), and pasta. Dill and capers add a bit of pop. If it's summer, To Be Eaten Only in Season Tomato Salad (page 138) is lovely on the side.

SECOND-DAY SALMON WITH LINGUINE

MAKES 1 SERVING

4 cups water

Salt

2 ounces linguine fini

About ⅓ cup cooked, flaked salmon

1 teaspoon freshly squeezed lemon juice

2 tablespoons chopped fresh dill

1 tablespoon crème fraîche

½ teaspoon extra-virgin olive oil

½ teaspoon rinsed and chopped capers (preferably salt-packed)

Freshly ground black pepper

1　In a large pot, bring the water and a healthy pinch of salt to a boil over high heat. Add the pasta and cook, stirring occasionally, until al dente, 6 to 8 minutes.

2　While the pasta cooks, put the salmon in a small bowl and douse it with the lemon juice.

3　Drain the pasta and transfer it to a medium bowl. Add the salmon, dill, crème fraîche, olive oil, capers, a pinch of salt, and a grind of pepper. Toss with tongs to combine well. Taste and adjust the seasoning, if desired. Serve warm.

I LEARNED TO MAKE this traditional Roman dish from friends in Frascati, which is about a half hour outside Rome, and I've taught it to friends and family in Paris, New York, and Philly. The key is quality ingredients. I'm partial to puree from San Marzano tomatoes or Rao's marinara and Ortiz tuna in extra-virgin olive oil. The rest is easy. A note about cookware: Your cast-iron skillet needs to be well seasoned if you are going to use it for tomato sauce. Otherwise, the acid in the tomatoes will react with the iron and could discolor your sauce or give it a metallic taste.

PASTA WITH TUNA (FROM ROME WITH LOVE) MAKES 1 SERVING

5 cups water

Salt

2 cups rigatoni

2½ teaspoons extra-virgin olive oil

2 garlic cloves, minced

2 cups tomato puree or marinara sauce

½ teaspoon dried oregano, plus more as needed

1 (4-ounce) can tuna in extra-virgin olive oil (preferably Ortiz brand), undrained

Freshly grated Parmesan cheese, for serving (optional)

1   In a large pot, bring the water and a healthy pinch of salt to a boil over high heat. Add the pasta and cook, stirring occasionally, until al dente, about 13 minutes.

2   Meanwhile, heat the olive oil in a large cast-iron skillet over medium heat, tilting the pan to coat the bottom. Add the garlic and cook, stirring, until fragrant, about 1 minute. Add the tomato puree and oregano and simmer for 2 to 3 minutes. Add the tuna and its oil, crushing the fish into bite-size pieces with the edge of a spoon or spatula. Taste and add salt and more oregano as needed.

3   When the pasta is done, drain it well, shaking the colander to get rid of all the water. Add the pasta to the skillet and stir to coat it with the sauce. Transfer it to a bowl, sprinkle Parmesan on top, if desired, and serve hot.

ONE OF THE MOST well-known dishes in Japanese cuisine, sashimi is thinly sliced raw food—usually fish, served without rice. In Tahiti my friends prepared a different version, which turns out to be a great recipe for one.

SASHIMI À LA TAHITIENNE   MAKES 1 SERVING

FOR THE RICE:

½ cup white rice

1 cup water

Salt

1 teaspoon grape seed oil

FOR THE VINAIGRETTE:

1 tablespoon freshly squeezed lime juice

1 tablespoon toasted sesame oil

2 teaspoons grape seed oil

2 teaspoons soy sauce

1½ teaspoons minced fresh ginger

1 teaspoon minced garlic

1 teaspoon Dijon mustard

TO FINISH THE SASHIMI:

¼ pound sushi-grade yellowfin tuna, cut into ¼-inch slices

Juice of ½ lime

½ cup finely chopped cabbage

1 tablespoon thinly sliced scallions

1   FOR THE RICE: In a fine-mesh sieve, rinse the rice under cold running water. (This eliminates excess starch, which would make the rice sticky.) Drain.

2   In a small saucepan, combine the rice, water, a pinch of salt, and the oil. Bring it to a boil, decrease the heat to maintain a simmer, and cook, covered, until the water is absorbed and the rice is tender, 12 to 15 minutes.

3   FOR THE VINAIGRETTE: While the rice cooks, whisk the lime juice, sesame oil, grape seed oil, soy sauce, ginger, garlic, and mustard in a small bowl.

4   TO FINISH THE SASHIMI: Put the tuna in another small bowl and squeeze the lime juice over it. When the rice is done, scoop it onto a serving plate. Spread the cabbage over it, arrange the tuna on top, and pour the vinaigrette over all. Sprinkle with the scallions and serve.

EAT MORE ASPARAGUS

"Recall that whatever lofty things you might accomplish today, you will do them only because you first ate something that grew out of dirt."

—Barbara Kingsolver

"Eat more vegetables" tops just about any list of things you can do to enhance your health. Ideally, those vegetables will be locally and organically grown for maximum nutrition and minimum pesticide exposure. With recipes ranging from Lemony White Bean Soup (page 120) to Roasted Vegetables with Tahini Vinaigrette (page 135), Hot Pink Hummus (page 146), and the best-ever Summer Vacation Sesame Noodles and Sugar Snap Peas (page 127), this chapter is for vegetarians, carnivores, and Meatless Monday people alike.

I MADE WHITE BEAN SOUP for the first time at my parents' home back in the early aughts, when we were on a cannellini-bean kick. We were concerned with getting enough protein and eating foods that satiate for several hours. Turns out beans do the trick. The soup came out better than I expected, and this version, brightened with lemon juice, is even better. It makes a fast, filling meal on its own, and it also goes well with a Lamb Burger (page 83). Be sure to let the cooked ingredients cool slightly before pureeing them. I learned the hard way that putting boiling-hot liquid in the blender can crack the glass container.

LEMONY WHITE BEAN SOUP

MAKES 1 SERVING

1 tablespoon extra-virgin olive oil

1 garlic clove, minced

1 (15½-ounce) can cannellini beans, drained

1 cup chicken or vegetable stock

Juice of 1 lemon

Salt

Freshly ground black pepper

1   In a medium saucepan, heat the oil over medium heat, tipping the pan to coat the bottom. Add the garlic and cook, stirring, until fragrant, about 1 minute. Add the beans and stock, raise the heat to high, and bring the ingredients to a boil. Decrease the heat and simmer for 2 to 3 minutes. Remove the pan from the heat and let the mixture cool for about 5 minutes.

2   Pour the contents of the saucepan into a blender and add the lemon juice, a pinch of salt, and a grind of pepper. Pulse to combine the ingredients and then blend on high speed until pureed, stopping the machine a time or two to stir, if necessary. Taste and adjust the seasoning, if desired. If it isn't hot enough, return the soup to the pot and reheat it. Pour it into a bowl and serve.

MANY VEGETABLES ARE MORE nutritious eaten raw, but not carrots. Cooking the orange sticks triples the amount of beta-carotene (antioxidant and protector of cells) that they deliver. I like to balance their earthy sweetness with spice and acidity, in this case with hot curry and lemon juice. Give the soup a creamy, tangy finish with labneh, a super-thick strained yogurt that you can buy in many supermarkets or make yourself with the recipe that follows. This pairs beautifully with Lamb I Love You: Chops (page 89).

CURRY-CARROT SOUP

MAKES 2 SERVINGS

1 tablespoon extra-virgin olive oil

1 garlic clove, minced

3 medium carrots, peeled and chopped (2 cups)

2 cups chicken or vegetable stock

¼ to ½ teaspoon hot curry powder

Juice of 1 lemon

Salt

Freshly ground black pepper

1 tablespoon labneh, for garnish (optional; recipe follows)

1 In a medium saucepan, heat the oil over medium heat, tilting the pan to coat the bottom. Add the garlic and cook, stirring, until fragrant, about 1 minute. Add the carrots and stock, raise the heat to high, and bring the mixture to a boil. Decrease the heat to maintain a simmer and cook, covered, until the carrots are very tender, 15 to 20 minutes. Let cool for about 5 minutes.

2 Transfer the carrot mixture to a blender along with the curry powder, lemon juice, a couple of pinches of salt, and a grind or two of pepper. Pulse to combine the ingredients and then process on high until the soup is smooth, about 2 minutes. Taste and add more salt or lemon juice, if necessary. If the soup isn't hot enough, return it to the pot and reheat. Garnish with the labneh, if desired, and serve.

LABNEH   MAKES ABOUT ⅓ CUP

Besides being a terrific garnish for creamy soups, labneh is great spread on toasted pita and finished with extra-virgin olive oil, or za'atar, a Middle Eastern spice blend.

⅛ teaspoon freshly squeezed lemon juice

Salt

6 ounces plain yogurt (goat's milk or cow's milk)

1 Stir the lemon juice and a pinch of salt into the yogurt. Line a large sieve with dampened cheesecloth and fit the sieve over an empty bowl.

2 Scrape the yogurt into the sieve and set it in the refrigerator for at least 24 hours. Discard the liquid that has drained from the yogurt. Transfer the labneh to a covered container and refrigerate. It will keep well for a week or more.

SOMETIMES I'M IMPATIENT and want a fast, hot dinner. Enter pasta. But I know that no meal is complete without a vegetable—thus the kale. This cruciferous green is packed with so much goodness I feel like it makes up for the bag of cookies I sometimes eat for lunch. Depending on what's hanging around in the fridge, I might add slivered sun-dried tomatoes or chopped anchovies. Bacon is great, too.

PASTA WITH KALE (THE EASIEST WAY TO EAT A SUPERFOOD)

MAKES 1 SERVING

3 cups water

Salt

1 cup penne

1 tablespoon extra-virgin olive oil

½ cup sliced red onion

2 cups chopped kale (thick ribs discarded)

1 tablespoon pine nuts

½ cup halved cherry tomatoes

½ cup freshly grated Parmesan cheese

1 teaspoon rinsed capers (preferably salt-packed; optional)

1 Add the water and a healthy pinch of salt to a medium saucepan and bring it to a boil over high heat. Add the pasta and cook until al dente, 10 to 12 minutes.

2 While the pasta cooks, heat the olive oil in a 10-inch cast-iron skillet over medium heat, tilting the pan to cover the bottom. Add the onion, kale, and a pinch of salt and cook, stirring occasionally, until the kale is wilted and the onions are soft, 5 to 8 minutes.

3 Meanwhile, in a small pan, toast the pine nuts over medium heat, shaking the pan often, until golden brown, 2 to 3 minutes.

4 Drain the pasta well and put it in a medium bowl. Add the kale mixture, tomatoes, cheese, and capers, if desired, and toss with tongs to combine. Top with the pine nuts. Serve hot.

PERHAPS YOU'VE BEEN ON a bit of a junk food spree—cookies for breakfast, chips for lunch, cake for supper. (It happens to the best of us.) You're ready to clean up your act, and you know vegetables are a good way to start. Look no further than this veggie-packed soup with a nutritional profile as vibrant as its hot pink color. Beets bring betalains and carrots have beta-carotene, two phytonutrients that are thought to block oxidative damage in the body. (In other words, they're antioxidants.) A dollop of labneh is the perfect finishing touch, and if you like a little crunch, sprinkle a few crushed toasted hazelnuts on top.

BEET-APPLE-CARROT POTAGE (VITAMIN SOUP) MAKES 1 SERVING

1 tablespoon extra-virgin olive oil

2 shallots, minced

1 garlic clove, minced

1 cup peeled and chopped red beets

1 cup peeled and chopped apple

1 carrot, peeled and chopped

1 cup water

3 tablespoons freshly squeezed lemon juice

Salt

Freshly ground black pepper

Labneh, homemade (page 122) or purchased, for serving

3 hazelnuts, toasted and crushed (optional)

1   In a medium saucepan, heat the oil over medium heat, tipping the pan to coat the bottom. Add the shallots and cook, stirring occasionally, until soft, 3 to 4 minutes. Add the garlic and cook, stirring, until fragrant, about 1 minute.

2   Add the beets, apple, carrot, and water to the pan, raise the heat to high, and bring the mixture to a boil. Decrease the heat to maintain a simmer and cook, covered, until the ingredients are tender when pierced with a fork, 15 to 20 minutes. Remove the pan from the heat and let the mixture cool for about 5 minutes.

3   Pour the contents of the pan into a blender and add the lemon juice, a pinch of salt, and a grind of pepper. Pulse to combine the ingredients and then blend on high speed until pureed, stopping the machine a time or two to stir if necessary. Taste and adjust the seasoning, if desired. If the soup has cooled too much, return it to the pot to reheat. Pour it into a bowl and garnish with a spoonful of labneh and a hint of freshly ground pepper. Sprinkle with the hazelnuts, if desired.

RISOTTO IS THE CAKE of dinners. Think about it: You take flour, sugar, butter, eggs, and leavening, you mix, you bake, and you end up with glorious cake. Likewise with risotto, you combine a few humble ingredients and produce a divine dish. I make it mainly in the winter when I want a cozy, creamy, melty meal. Sautéed spinach is great on the side. Unlike other risotto recipes you may have tried, mine does not require heating the liquid and adding it a little at a time. It does, however, involve standing at the stove stirring for 20 to 30 minutes straight, so make sure you've got a great playlist on before you start. The next day, form leftover risotto into patties, cook them until lightly browned in olive oil, and serve with a salad.

SHIITAKE RISOTTO   MAKES 4 SERVINGS

2 tablespoons plus 1 teaspoon extra-virgin olive oil

¾ cup diced onion

1 cup Arborio rice

2 cups chicken or vegetable stock

1 cup white wine

1 cup thinly sliced shiitake mushroom caps

½ cup freshly grated Parmesan cheese

2 teaspoons white truffle oil (optional)

Salt

Freshly ground black pepper

1   Heat 2 tablespoons of the oil in a large saucepan over medium heat, tilting the pan to coat the bottom. Add the onion and cook, stirring occasionally, until translucent, about 5 minutes. Add the rice and cook, stirring, until the grains are coated with oil and have become slightly translucent, about 4 minutes.

2   Stir in the stock, raise the heat to high, and bring the mixture to a boil. Add the wine, adjust the heat to maintain a simmer, and cook, stirring constantly until the rice is tender and creamy, 20 to 30 minutes.

3   In a small skillet, heat the remaining 1 teaspoon oil over medium-high heat. Add the mushrooms and cook, stirring, until tender and lightly browned, 4 to 5 minutes.

4   Stir the shiitakes into the risotto, along with the Parmesan, truffle oil (if desired), a pinch or two of salt, and a grind of pepper. Taste, adjust the seasoning, if desired, and serve.

MARTHA'S VINEYARD IS A summer tradition for my family. When we're there, our routine revolves around going to the beach, watching lots of movies, and eating tons of delicious food. Morning Glory Farm is my favorite place to pick up fresh peas for this dish, and they make noodles that inspired this recipe. We usually eat this with Pan-Seared Tuna (page 103).

SUMMER VACATION SESAME NOODLES AND SUGAR SNAP PEAS

MAKES 1 SERVING

4 cups water

2 ounces spaghetti

Salt

2 tablespoons toasted sesame oil

1 tablespoon chopped fresh ginger

3 teaspoons soy sauce

1 teaspoon light brown sugar

1 teaspoon sesame seeds

2 cups sugar snap peas, trimmed

1 In a large pot, bring the water to a boil over high heat. Add the spaghetti and a pinch of salt. Cook, stirring occasionally, until al dente, about 10 minutes.

2 While the pasta cooks, combine the sesame oil, ginger, soy sauce, brown sugar, and sesame seeds in a medium bowl. Whisk to combine and set aside.

3 About 2 minutes before the pasta is done, toss the peas into the pasta water to blanch.

4 Drain the pasta and peas well and add them to the bowl. Toss the mixture with tongs, coating the pasta with the sauce. Serve hot, at room temperature, or chilled.

I'M A FAN OF shiitake mushrooms; they kind of remind me of meat. I also love polenta, which remind me of grits. Shiitakes and polenta come together here, crowned with a poached egg, in a mouthwatering dish. Watercress, Cilantro, and Arugula Salad (page 156) would be lovely on the side.

POLENTA WITH SHIITAKE MUSHROOMS   MAKES 1 SERVING

6 cups water

½ cup polenta

¼ teaspoon salt

1 tablespoon distilled white vinegar

1 large egg

2 teaspoons extra-virgin olive oil

½ cup chopped shiitake mushroom caps

1 teaspoon white truffle oil (optional)

½ cup freshly grated Parmesan cheese

1   Bring 2 cups of the water to a boil in a medium saucepan over high heat. Add the polenta and salt, whisking constantly for 2 minutes. Decrease the heat and simmer, stirring from time to time, until the polenta is thick and pulls away from the side of the pan when stirred, 30 to 40 minutes.

2   About 15 minutes before the polenta is done, bring the remaining 4 cups water to a boil in a large saucepan. Add the vinegar and adjust the heat to a brisk simmer. Break the egg into a small bowl and pour it into the simmering water. Poach until the white turns opaque, 3 to 4 minutes. Remove the egg with a slotted spoon and place it on a clean kitchen towel to drain.

3   In a small skillet, heat 1 teaspoon of the olive oil over medium-high heat. Add the mushrooms and a pinch of salt and cook, stirring, until they're tender and slightly browned, 4 to 5 minutes.

4   When the polenta is done, stir in the mushrooms, truffle oil (if desired), and remaining 1 teaspoon olive oil. Taste and adjust the seasoning, if desired. Transfer to a bowl, top with the poached egg and Parmesan, and serve.

ON NEW YEAR'S DAY, when I was a kid, my mom and I would get out needles and thread and make miniature pillows filled with black-eyed peas for good luck. Today, I'm more likely to use the two-tone legumes in my New Year's menu. This is my interpretation of hoppin' John, the traditional Southern good-luck dish. Instead of rice, I cook the peas with sweet potatoes, and add a hit of habanero chile pepper. I serve the dish with Curry Sautéed Kale (page 136) and basmati rice. If you forget to soak the peas overnight, give them a 10-minute head start in the pot with the water before adding the other ingredients.

DOWN-HOME SPICY BLACK-EYED PEAS AND SWEET POTATOES

MAKES 1 SERVING

2 teaspoons extra-virgin olive oil

1 cup chopped onion

1 garlic clove, minced

2 cups water

½ cup black-eyed peas, soaked for 6 to 8 hours and drained

2 tablespoons chopped, dry-packed sun-dried tomatoes

½ teaspoon minced habanero chile

¼ teaspoon salt

1 cup peeled and chopped sweet potato

Freshly ground black pepper

1 Heat the oil in a large saucepan over medium heat, tilting the pan to coat the bottom. Add the onion and garlic and cook, stirring occasionally, until translucent, about 5 minutes.

2 Add the water, peas, tomatoes, chile, and salt. Raise the heat to high, bring the mixture to a boil, and decrease the heat to maintain a simmer. Cook, covered, for 30 minutes, stirring from time to time and adding more water if the pan becomes too dry.

3 Add the sweet potato and cook until the sweet potatoes and peas are tender, 15 to 20 minutes.

4 Taste and add a few grinds of pepper and more salt, if needed. Serve hot.

WHILE PERCHED ON a stool at the bar eating harissa-spiced ribs at Il Buco, a perfect Italian restaurant on Bond Street in NoHo, I had an epiphany about dining out alone: It's incredibly freeing. You can eat with your hands or moan with pleasure, and no one is likely to notice or care. If you're really lucky—like I was that night—you'll meet the chef and talk him out of his recipe for the tastiest carrots on earth. I've adapted it here, omitting hard-to-find black garlic. The carrots are still terrific, especially with lamb, and also make a nice addition to salads.

BEST CARROTS EVER (ALLA IL BUCO) MAKES 1 SERVING

6 baby carrots

2 tablespoons extra-virgin olive oil

1 garlic clove, minced

Salt

Juice of 1 lime

1 Preheat the oven to 375°F.

2 Place the carrots in a small casserole dish, douse with the olive oil, sprinkle with the garlic and salt, and roast for 16 to 20 minutes, until tender when pierced with a fork.

3 Drizzle the carrots with the lime juice and serve warm or at room temperature.

IN 2005 I WENT to Ethiopia to write about its astonishingly delicious food culture. I met up there with writers Matt and Ted Lee and chef Marcus Samuelsson, who, along with his friends Hanna Shiferaw and Workafes Woldemariam, took us to some of the best restaurants in Addis Ababa. One of the highlights of my time in Addis was a trip to Merkato, the biggest open market in Africa, where we visited a berbere shop. Berbere is a spice blend that permeates Ethiopian cuisine. It contains chiles, ginger, garlic, fenugreek seeds, peppercorns, allspice, cardamom, cloves, paprika, and more. It smells and tastes divine—hot, earthy, and pungent all at once. I use it to season roasted asparagus for a quick, flavorful vegetable side. The spice is also great on meat and fish. You can buy berbere from online retailers including spicetrekkers.com and at well-stocked spice shops.

BERBERE-ROASTED ASPARAGUS MAKES 1 SERVING

12 green asparagus spears

1 tablespoon extra-virgin olive oil

Berbere

Salt

1 Preheat the oven to 400°F. Cut off and discard the thick ends of the asparagus.

2 Place the asparagus on a baking sheet and drizzle with the olive oil. Sprinkle each spear with a generous pinch of berbere and a pinch of salt.

3 Roast the asparagus for 12 to 16 minutes, until bright green, slightly shriveled, and tender when pricked with a fork. Serve hot.

IN SOME FANTASY WORLD I might eat chocolate all day, but, truth be told, you can coax satisfying sweetness from vegetables when you roast them. The idea here is to make a big batch so you have veggies on hand through the week. They're delicious on their own or with rice, Roasted Salmon with Shiso and Sesame Maple Syrup (page 104), Lamb I Love You: Chops (page 89), or in frittatas, to name a few possible pairings. The vinaigrette is flavored with tahini, a thick, velvety paste made from sesame seeds.

ROASTED VEGETABLES WITH TAHINI VINAIGRETTE

MAKES 4 SERVINGS

FOR THE SALAD:

3 medium sweet potatoes, peeled and chopped

4 medium carrots, peeled and sliced

1 large red onion, thinly sliced

1 medium zucchini, halved and sliced

1 cup cherry tomatoes (optional)

2 garlic cloves, halved

Salt

Freshly ground black pepper

2 tablespoons extra-virgin olive oil

FOR THE VINAIGRETTE:

2 tablespoons tahini

2 teaspoons extra-virgin olive oil

Juice of 1 lemon

1 garlic clove, minced

Salt

1   Preheat the oven to 375°F.

2   FOR THE SALAD: Combine the sweet potatoes, carrots, onion, zucchini, tomatoes (if desired), and garlic in a large bowl. Sprinkle with several pinches of salt and grinds of pepper. Drizzle with the olive oil and toss with your hands to coat the vegetables.

3   Line a baking sheet with parchment paper and spread the vegetables on it in a single layer. Roast for 45 to 55 minutes, until the vegetables are tender and have begun to caramelize and turn slightly brown. Remove the pan from the oven and set it aside on a cooling rack.

4   FOR THE VINAIGRETTE: Combine the tahini, olive oil, lemon juice, garlic, and a pinch of salt in a small bowl and whisk until emulsified. Taste and adjust the seasoning, if desired.

5   When the vegetables are cool enough to handle, drizzle them with the vinaigrette and toss with your hands to coat. Serve warm or at room temperature. Refrigerate leftovers, covered, for up to 4 days.

IF THERE'S ONE VEGETABLE to eat, one green triple threat, kale is it. Check this out: One serving packs more calcium than a serving of milk and a ton more fiber than a slice of whole-grain bread, plus it's got vitamin C and is a member of the cancer-fighting cruciferous family. People, you can't go wrong with kale. For a vegan feast, pair this dish with Roasted Vegetables with Tahini Vinaigrette (page 135) or Down-Home Spicy Black-Eyed Peas and Sweet Potatoes (page 130). It's quite nice with meat, too, of course.

CURRY SAUTÉED KALE   MAKES 1 SERVING

2 teaspoons extra-virgin olive oil

½ cup thinly sliced onion

1 garlic clove, minced

2 cups finely chopped kale leaves (thick ribs discarded)

⅛ teaspoon hot curry powder

Salt

1   In a medium saucepan or skillet, heat the oil over medium heat, tilting the pan to coat the bottom. Add the onion and cook, stirring occasionally, until softened, 3 to 4 minutes. Add the garlic and cook, stirring, until fragrant, about 1 minute.

2   Stir in the kale and sprinkle with the curry powder and a pinch of salt. Cook, stirring, for a couple of minutes. Cover the pan and cook until the kale is wilted and bright green, 2 to 3 minutes. Taste and adjust the seasoning, if desired. Serve warm.

MY FAVORITE ITALIAN RESTAURANT in New York, Il Buco, serves an amazing take on Caesar salad made with *cavalo nero*, also known as lacinato kale, Tuscan kale, or dinosaur kale. When I attempted to replicate it, I ended up with something quite different but delicious. The key is to remove the coarse ribs from the kale before slicing it. Use your chef's knife or kitchen shears.

LET THEM EAT KALE! CAESAR SALAD

MAKES 1 SERVING

1 (2-ounce) can anchovies (preferably Roland brand)

2 tablespoons extra-virgin olive oil, plus more if needed

1 tablespoon finely chopped walnuts

1 garlic clove, minced

Juice of 1 lemon

3 cups finely sliced lacinato kale leaves (thick ribs discarded)

2 ounces Parmesan cheese, thinly sliced

1 Finely chop the anchovies and put them in a large bowl, along with the olive oil, walnuts, garlic, and lemon juice. Whisk to combine. Taste and add more olive oil or lemon juice if necessary.

2 Add the kale to the bowl and toss with your hands to coat it with the dressing, massaging the leaves to soften them. Add the Parmesan and toss again. Transfer to a plate and serve.

GO FOR THE MOST POTENT and healthful tomatoes out there: the grape or cherry variety. According to *Bon Appétit* magazine, the smaller varieties pack eighteen times more lycopene (a powerful antioxidant and protector of cells) than big tomatoes. Let's hear it for goodness in small packages! Petite tomatoes are also a single cook's friend because the portioning is so easy. (You'll never end up with a half a tomato losing flavor in the fridge.) This salad is terrific with any of the burgers on pages 83 to 86 or Kale and Blue Cheese Pizza (page 163). Pine nuts toast up nicely in just a few minutes in a dry skillet over medium heat. Toss them often and watch carefully, as they burn easily.

TO BE EATEN ONLY IN SEASON TOMATO SALAD MAKES 1 SERVING

2 cups halved cherry or grape tomatoes

½ cup diced feta cheese

¼ cup finely chopped fresh flat-leaf parsley

2 tablespoons pine nuts, toasted (see Note)

1 garlic clove, minced

Salt

2 teaspoons extra-virgin olive oil

1 In a medium bowl, combine the tomatoes, feta, parsley, pine nuts, garlic, and a few pinches of salt. Drizzle with the olive oil and toss with your hands to coat. Taste and adjust the seasoning, if desired, and serve.

Note: To toast the pine nuts, place them in a dry skillet over medium heat and stir the nuts continuously until they are slightly golden and release a faint, toasty aroma, 2 to 3 minutes.

ON FRIDAYS, I LOVE to go to the farmers' market around the corner from my apartment, buy the most vibrant-looking produce, and create a recipe on the fly. That's how I came up with this coleslaw. The purple-red color makes it a stunner. You'll be the envy of your office mates if you pack it into a mason jar and take it to work for lunch with a sandwich. It's also delicious with the burgers on pages 83 to 86.

MASON JAR RED CABBAGE SALAD MAKES 1 SERVING

2 tablespoons extra-virgin olive oil

2 teaspoons apple cider vinegar

3 pinches salt

2 cups thinly sliced red cabbage (about ¼ head)

1 carrot, peeled and thinly sliced

1 red beet, peeled, quartered, and thinly sliced

½ cup halved cherry tomatoes

¼ cup thinly sliced red onion

2 tablespoons coarsely chopped fresh basil

1 Combine the oil, vinegar, and salt in a medium bowl and whisk until emulsified.

2 Add the cabbage, carrot, beet, tomatoes, onion, and basil to the bowl. Toss with your hands to mix the vegetables and coat them with the dressing. Taste and adjust seasoning if desired. Serve immediately, or transfer to a covered container (preferably a mason jar) and refrigerate.

IMAGINE YOU'RE IN SPAIN, seated at a table on the terrace of a beautiful home in the green hills of Andalusia. Your host sets before you this salad, finished with zest from citrus that was grown on trees you can see in the distance. It looks simple enough, but the bitter greens, anise-flavored fennel, and bright burst of orange make your mouth happy. This salad is great alongside anything rich, including Grilled Blue Cheese with Curried Red Onions (page 42).

FENNEL, ARUGULA, AND ORANGE ZEST SALAD   MAKES 1 SERVING

2 tablespoons extra-virgin olive oil

1 garlic clove, minced

2 teaspoons balsamic vinegar

1 teaspoon Dijon mustard

½ teaspoon soy sauce

Salt

2 cups packed arugula

¾ cup thinly sliced fennel
(bulb only)

½ ounce Parmesan cheese,
thinly sliced

Grated zest of ½ orange

1   In a large bowl, whisk the olive oil, garlic, vinegar, mustard, soy sauce, and a pinch of salt until emulsified.

2   Add the arugula and fennel to the bowl and toss with your hands to coat.

3   Strew the Parmesan and orange zest over the salad. Transfer to a plate and serve immediately.

A PHOTO OF FINELY cut vegetables inspired this dish. It turns out that when you thinly slice a zucchini lengthwise, it's a total beauty—like a wide ribbon or vegetal pappardelle pasta. You don't need a mandoline to achieve the effect; a vegetable peeler does the job.

PHOTOGENIC SHAVED ZUCCHINI SALAD (MADE FOR INSTAGRAM) MAKES 1 SERVING

2 large zucchini

1 cup halved cherry tomatoes

⅓ cup pitted and chopped Kalamata olives

¼ cup diced feta cheese

1 tablespoon pine nuts, toasted (see Note)

3 tablespoons extra-virgin olive oil

1 tablespoon apple cider vinegar

1 tablespoon balsamic vinegar

1 garlic clove, minced

¼ teaspoon freshly ground black pepper

Salt

1   Trim the ends from the zucchini. Over a large bowl, shave them lengthwise into ribbons using a vegetable peeler. Add the tomatoes, olives, feta, and pine nuts, and set aside.

2   In a small jar with a tight-fitting lid, combine the oil, vinegars, garlic, pepper, and a pinch of salt. Shake vigorously until emulsified, about 1 minute.

3   Pour the dressing over the vegetables and cheese and toss with your hands to coat. Transfer to a plate and serve.

Note: To toast the pine nuts, place them in a dry skillet over medium heat and stir the nuts continuously until they are slightly golden and release a faint, toasty aroma, 2 to 3 minutes.

I WAS INTRODUCED TO Greek salad in the Plaka, the ancient neighborhood near the Acropolis in Athens. I fell in love with the combination of feta, olives, and oregano, and it has been a warm-weather favorite ever since. Serve this with Tarragon Roasted Chicken (page 92), pour yourself a glass of Retsina, and be transported.

GREEK SALAD (SHOUT-OUT TO THE PLAKA) MAKES 1 SERVING

2 tablespoons extra-virgin olive oil

2½ teaspoons red wine vinegar

½ teaspoon dried oregano

Salt

3 cups shredded romaine lettuce

1 cucumber, peeled and chopped

1 large tomato, chopped

⅓ cup chopped red onion

4 ounces feta cheese, diced

8 Kalamata olives, pitted and chopped

1 In a large bowl, combine the oil, vinegar, oregano, and a pinch of salt. Whisk until emulsified.

2 Add the lettuce, cucumber, tomato, onion, feta, and olives. Toss with your hands to coat the salad with the vinaigrette. Transfer to a plate and serve.

THIS SPREAD REMINDS ME of hummus because of the tahini and lemon juice, but the beets elevate it with their earthy sweetness and vivid color. Add toasted pita, feta, and olives, and you've got yourself a light meal or a fine accompaniment for Roasted Vegetables with Tahini Vinaigrette (page 135).

HOT PINK HUMMUS (ROASTED BEET SPREAD) MAKES 1 SERVING

2 medium beets, scrubbed

2 tablespoons plus 1 teaspoon extra-virgin olive oil

½ cup freshly squeezed lemon juice

2 tablespoons tahini

1 garlic clove, minced

Salt

1   Preheat the oven to 400°F.

2   Rub the beets with 1 teaspoon of the olive oil, wrap them in aluminum foil, and put them in the oven to roast for about 1 hour, or until tender when pierced with a fork. Let them sit on a rack until cool enough to handle.

3   Unwrap the beets, pull off the skin with a paring knife, and cut them into quarters. Add them to a blender with the remaining 2 tablespoons olive oil, the lemon juice, tahini, garlic, and a pinch of salt. Pulse to combine the ingredients and then blend on high speed until smooth.

4   Taste for seasoning and add a little extra salt if needed. Serve at room temperature.

ENTERTAINING FRIENDS

"A person is a person through other people."

—Desmond Tutu

olo living is the theme of this book, and there's nothing more important to most singles I know than spending time with friends. That's why I've devoted this chapter to entertaining. Hospitality is simply opening your door to the people you love and taking care of them. It's an expression of generosity that requires no fancy menu. It's all in the welcoming: A smile. A kiss. A beverage. Something to eat. Good conversation. That's all it takes to entertain. Anyone can do it. And we should all do it more often. This is what homes and food are for.

The recipes in this chapter serve from two to eight people, from an intimate dinner with a romantic interest to a big meal for friends. Weekend brunches are my favorite way of entertaining. They're more casual (thus less stressful) than dinner parties, and because Saturday or Sunday stretches out before you, friends can linger for hours, making brunch more satisfying socially. Brunch is also a perfect opportunity to serve my favorite food group—waffles, both savory and sweet—and you'll find four fabulous versions here.

THIS SOUP IS INSPIRED by one I tasted at Metropolitan Bakery, my go-to spot in Philadelphia for scones, cookies, bread, and, sometimes, lunch. Thick and hearty, it combines four of my favorite ingredients: sweet potatoes, curry, cilantro, and coconut. Invite a couple of friends over, put Tarragon Roasted Chicken (page 92) in the oven, and serve this to start.

SPICY COCONUT–SWEET POTATO SOUP

MAKES 4 SERVINGS

1 tablespoon extra-virgin olive oil

2 celery ribs, chopped

1 cup chopped onion

1 shallot, minced

3 cups coconut milk

2 cups peeled and chopped sweet potato (about 3 medium sweet potatoes)

1 cup peeled and chopped carrot (about 2 medium carrots)

½ cup water

2-inch piece fresh ginger, peeled and chopped

¾ teaspoon hot curry powder

¼ teaspoon salt

2 tablespoons chopped fresh cilantro

1 tablespoon chopped fresh chives

1 In a large saucepan or soup pot, heat the oil over medium heat, tilting the pan to coat the bottom. Add the celery, onion, and shallot and cook, stirring occasionally, until the onion and shallot are translucent, about 5 minutes.

2 Add the coconut milk, sweet potato, carrot, water, ginger, curry powder, and salt to the pot. Raise the heat to high, bring the mixture to a boil, and decrease the heat to maintain a simmer. Cook, covered, until the vegetables are very tender, about 30 minutes. Take the pan off the heat for 5 to 10 minutes to allow the soup to cool slightly.

3 Working in batches, process the vegetables, cooking liquid, cilantro, and chives in a blender until pureed. Taste and add more salt if necessary. If the soup isn't hot enough, return it to the pot and reheat. Serve hot.

I MADE THIS ON a whim for a family road trip to Maine. My mom loved it and said I should put it in my cookbook, so here it is. Bring it to a potluck, or put it on the table the next time you grill burgers for friends. It can be made up to an hour ahead.

ROAD TRIP STRING BEAN AND TOMATO SALAD   MAKES 3 SERVINGS

4 cups water

6 to 8 ounces string beans, trimmed

Salt

1 tablespoon extra-virgin olive oil

1 garlic clove, minced

2 teaspoons balsamic vinegar

Freshly ground black pepper

1 cup halved cherry tomatoes

1   In a large saucepan, bring the water to a boil. Add the string beans and a pinch of salt and cook until bright green but still crunchy, 2 to 3 minutes. Drain and set aside.

2   In a medium bowl, combine the olive oil, garlic, vinegar, a pinch of salt, and a grind of pepper. Whisk until emulsified.

3   Add the beans and tomatoes to the bowl, tossing with your hands to coat the vegetables with the dressing. Serve at room temperature.

THIS SALAD SAYS SUMMER to me. First, you've got juicy, red watermelon. Second, there are jalapeños, so you know something exciting is about to happen. Add tomatoes for acidity, onion for a bit of bite, mint for refreshment, and feta for a hit of salty creaminess, and you've got a great addition to any summer party or cookout. It's also lovely with a Lamb Burger (page 83) and Lemony White Bean Soup (page 120).

JALAPEÑO-WATERMELON SALAD

MAKES 3 SERVINGS

3 tablespoons extra-virgin olive oil

1 tablespoon apple cider vinegar

1 tablespoon balsamic vinegar

1 garlic clove, minced

½ teaspoon salt

¼ teaspoon freshly ground black pepper

3 cups arugula

2 cups diced seedless watermelon

½ cup halved cherry tomatoes

¼ cup diced red onion

2 tablespoons diced feta cheese

2 tablespoons minced fresh mint

1 tablespoon seeded and minced jalapeño

1 In a large bowl, combine the olive oil, vinegars, garlic, salt, and pepper. Whisk until emulsified.

2 Add the arugula, watermelon, tomatoes, onion, feta, mint, and jalapeño. Toss with your hands to combine well. Serve immediately.

WATERCRESS IS ONE OF my favorite greens. It looks so adorably dainty, but it packs a peppery bite, plus it's practically got the alphabet of vitamins and other nutrients (it topped a William Paterson University list of "powerhouse fruits and vegetables"). Put this refreshing salad together while Kale and Blue Cheese Pizza (page 163) or Puffy Mushroom Tart with Truffled Fontina Cheese (page 165) is in the oven for movie-at-home night with your friends.

WATERCRESS, CILANTRO, AND ARUGULA SALAD MAKES 3 SERVINGS

2 tablespoons extra-virgin olive oil

1 tablespoon freshly squeezed lemon juice

1 tablespoon chopped Kalamata olives

1 garlic clove, minced

1 teaspoon Dijon mustard

½ teaspoon soy sauce

¼ teaspoon rinsed and chopped capers (preferably salt-packed)

2 cups watercress

2 cups arugula

½ cup fresh cilantro leaves, picked from the stem

1 tablespoon chopped fresh dill

1 tablespoon pine nuts, toasted (see Note)

Grated zest of ½ orange

4 teaspoons golden raisins

1 In a large bowl, combine the olive oil, lemon juice, olives, garlic, mustard, soy sauce, and capers. Whisk until the ingredients emulsify.

2 Add the watercress, arugula, cilantro, dill, pine nuts, orange zest, and raisins. Toss with your hands to mix and coat with the dressing. Serve immediately.

Note: To toast the pine nuts, place them in a skillet over medium heat and stir the nuts continuously until they are slightly golden and release a faint, toasty aroma, 2 to 3 minutes.

THIS IS A RIDICULOUSLY SIMPLE recipe. Buy a jar of apple butter (I like Dutch Country Kettle brand), and simmer it with a knob of butter while you prep the Brussels sprouts. Roast the sprouts and bacon, top them with the apple butter mixture, pop the casserole back in the oven, and wait for one of the best smells ever—caramelized bacon. I love serving this for brunch with Sweet Potato Belgian Waffles (page 170). It's so good, you won't believe you made it. Neither will your friends—but they'll be psyched to eat at your house all the time.

BACON WITH BRUSSELS SPROUTS AND APPLE BUTTER

MAKES 4 TO 6 SERVINGS

2 cups apple butter

2 tablespoons butter

2 pounds Brussels sprouts

8 bacon strips, halved

Salt

1 tablespoon extra-virgin olive oil

1   Preheat the oven to 400°F.

2   Put the apple butter and butter in a small saucepan and heat over low heat, stirring occasionally, until the butter is melted and the mixture is well combined, about 5 minutes.

3   Meanwhile, trim off the bottoms of the Brussels sprouts, and cut them in half.

4   Put the Brussels sprouts and bacon in a shallow casserole dish and sprinkle with a pinch of salt. Drizzle with the olive oil and set in the oven to roast for 20 minutes.

5   Remove the casserole from the oven, pour the apple butter mixture on top, and return it to the oven for 15 to 20 minutes, until the Brussels sprouts are soft when pierced with a fork. Serve hot or at room temperature.

YOU'RE BESOTTED. You dragged yourself to a party you didn't want to go to, and you met someone at the punch bowl. He or she is drop-dead gorgeous and a great conversationalist. Sparks flew. There was so much laughter. A connection like you haven't felt in ages. You've been seeing each other for a few weeks, and now it's time to do something cozy, impressive, and homemade. Enter this mouthwatering recipe: sensual ribbons of fresh pasta bathed in a savory meat sauce. Serve this alongside Fennel, Arugula, and Orange Zest Salad (page 141) or Best Carrots Ever (page 131), open a bottle of robust red wine, and make merry.

PAPPARDELLE AND BEEF RAGÙ (YOU'RE IN LOVE PASTA)   MAKES 2 SERVINGS

1 tablespoon extra-virgin olive oil

2 garlic cloves, minced

½ pound lean, grass-fed ground beef

⅛ teaspoon salt

Freshly ground black pepper

4 cups water

¼ cup red wine

3 tablespoons tomato paste (preferably San Marzano)

2 teaspoons butter

5 fresh sage leaves, finely chopped

4 ounces fresh pappardelle

2 teaspoons freshly grated Parmesan cheese (optional)

1   In a large cast-iron skillet, heat the oil over low heat. Add the garlic and cook, stirring, until fragrant, about 1 minute. Add the ground beef, salt, and a grind of pepper and cook, stirring, until lightly browned, about 5 minutes, crumbling the meat with a wooden spoon.

2   Meanwhile, put the water on to boil in a large saucepan. Add a pinch of salt to the water.

3   When the meat is browned, stir in the wine, tomato paste, butter, and sage. Bring the mixture to a simmer, stirring occasionally.

4   Add the pasta to the boiling water and cook until just tender, 2 to 3 minutes. Drain well and stir the pasta into the meat sauce. Taste to check for seasoning and add more salt if necessary. Divide the pasta between 2 plates and serve hot. Top with the Parmesan, if desired.

(a feast for your eyes and taste buds)

I NEEDED SOME VISUAL fodder for my blog, so I hosted a brunch for my posse, and this risotto was a hit. It was, by far, the prettiest thing we ate—and it tasted great, too. So did the rest of the feast, which included Fennel, Arugula, and Orange Zest Salad (page 141), and Cornbread Waffles with Jalapeños and Sun-Dried Tomatoes (page 168).

LEMONY KALE RISOTTO   MAKES 4 SERVINGS

2 tablespoons plus 2 teaspoons extra-virgin olive oil

¾ cup diced onion

1 cup Arborio rice

2 cups chicken or vegetable stock

1 cup white wine

½ cup plus 4 tablespoons freshly grated Parmesan cheese

½ teaspoon salt

Freshly ground black pepper

2 cups thinly sliced kale leaves (thick ribs discarded)

Grated zest of 1 lemon

1 In a large saucepan, heat 2 tablespoons of the olive oil over medium heat. Add the onion and cook, stirring occasionally, until translucent, about 5 minutes. Add the rice, stir to coat it with olive oil, and cook until the grains are slightly translucent, about 4 minutes.

2 Stir in 1 cup of the stock and bring the mixture to a boil over high heat. Add the wine and adjust the heat to maintain a simmer. Cook, stirring constantly, until the rice absorbs all the liquid. Add the remaining 1 cup stock and cook, still stirring, until the rice becomes tender and creamy, 25 to 30 minutes total.

3 Stir in ½ cup of the Parmesan, the salt, and a few grinds of pepper. Taste and add more salt if necessary. Simmer for 5 more minutes.

4 While the risotto finishes, heat the remaining 2 teaspoons olive oil in a large cast-iron skillet over medium-high heat, tilting the pan to coat the bottom. Add the kale and a pinch of salt and cook, stirring occasionally, until wilted and bright green, 2 to 3 minutes.

5 Divide the risotto among 4 shallow bowls. Sprinkle one-quarter of the remaining Parmesan cheese over each portion and add a little lemon zest on top. Arrange the kale over the risotto. Serve hot.

I LOVE MAKING PIZZA for friends, and I've learned that once you prepare the dough, the rest is quick and easy. Given the 3-hour rising time, you really need to plan ahead, but this recipe yields enough dough for two pizzas—a head start on a second meal. The dough recipe is adapted from one that Sam Sifton developed for the *New York Times* (with cues from Anthony Falco of Roberta's Pizza in Brooklyn), and the topping is inspired by a pizza I had at ABC Kitchen in Manhattan. I think of it as a cooked salad pizza with blue cheese. After you master dough making, you can have fun improvising your own toppings. Complete the meal with To Be Eaten Only in Season Tomato Salad (page 138) or clusters of grapes and lots of red wine—I vote for Lambrusco.

KALE AND BLUE CHEESE PIZZA

MAKES 1 (3-SERVING) PIZZA, PLUS DOUGH FOR A SECOND PIZZA

FOR THE DOUGH:

2 cups plus 2 tablespoons all-purpose flour, plus more for dusting

1 teaspoon salt

1 cup warm water

1 teaspoon extra-virgin olive oil

¾ teaspoon active dry yeast

1 FOR THE DOUGH: Combine the flour and salt in a large bowl and whisk to mix.

2 Stir the warm water, olive oil, and yeast together in a small bowl. Pour the mixture over the dry ingredients and use your hands to mix them. Knead for about 3 minutes in the bowl. Set the dough aside to rest for 15 minutes.

3 Knead the dough for 3 more minutes in the bowl. Cover the bowl with a clean, damp kitchen towel and set the dough aside to rise at room temperature until almost doubled in size, 3 to 4 hours.

. . . *continued*

FOR THE TOPPING:

1 large bunch kale (preferably lacinato)

6 ounces blue cheese, sliced or crumbled

2 teaspoons extra-virgin olive oil

Salt

Freshly ground black pepper

¼ cup snipped fresh dill

4   FOR THE TOPPING: Preheat the oven to its highest setting. Fold each kale leaf in half and pull out the center rib. Discard the ribs and chop the leaves finely. Set aside.

5   Once the dough has doubled, punch it down and divide it into 2 equal portions. Dust one of them well with flour, place it in a food-storage bag, and refrigerate for later use. (It can be refrigerated for up to 24 hours or frozen for up to 1 month.)

6   Spread flour on a work surface and use your hands or a well-floured rolling pin to stretch and shape the other piece of dough into a rectangle about 9 by 11 inches. Slide it onto a baking sheet.

7   Top the dough evenly with the blue cheese and bake for 8 to 10 minutes, until the cheese is completely melted and the dough is a light golden color.

8   While the pizza bakes, heat the olive oil in a cast-iron skillet over medium-high heat, tilting the pan to coat the bottom. Add the kale and salt and pepper to taste. Cook, stirring occasionally, until the kale is wilted and bright green. Taste and adjust the seasoning, if desired.

9   Remove the pizza from the oven. Top with the kale, sprinkle with the dill, slice, and serve hot.

PIZZA IS MY GO-TO MEAL for large groups, but sometimes you need a quick brunch option. Cue the frozen puff pastry dough. Oozy, gooey, cheesy, crunchy, and delicious, this tart is a crowd-pleaser that's a snap to make. Serve it with Fennel, Arugula, and Orange Zest Salad (page 141).

PUFFY MUSHROOM TART WITH TRUFFLED FONTINA CHEESE

MAKES 4 SERVINGS

1 (11-inch square) sheet puff pastry dough, thawed according to package directions

1 teaspoon extra-virgin olive oil

2 cups thinly sliced shiitake mushroom caps

1 cup thinly sliced button mushrooms

Salt

1½ cups chopped truffled Fontina cheese

1 Preheat the oven to 375°F.

2 Arrange the puff pastry dough on a baking sheet and bake for 15 minutes, or until light golden.

3 Meanwhile, heat the olive oil in a cast-iron skillet over medium-high heat, tilting the pan to coat the bottom. Add all the mushrooms, sprinkle lightly with salt, and cook, stirring, until they have cooked down and their liquid has evaporated, 8 to 10 minutes. Taste and add more salt if needed.

4 Remove the pastry from the oven. Use a small, sharp knife to cut through the top layers, about 2 inches from the edge, all the way around. Use a spatula or the back of a spoon to press down the pastry that has puffed up in the middle. Spread the mushrooms evenly in the center of the pastry, leaving a 2-inch border, and scatter the cheese over them.

5 Return the tart to the oven and bake for 8 to 10 minutes, until the pastry is golden brown and the cheese is melted. Cut into squares and serve warm.

WHEN YOU NEED A speedy brunch or supper dish for friends, think frittata. It takes only about 15 minutes to prepare and 20 minutes to cook. Plus, you can add almost anything to the eggs—leftover pasta, stale bread, chorizo, tomatoes—so it's a great way to get creative while making a filling meal. Greek Salad (page 144) or Spicy Coconut–Sweet Potato Soup (page 152) would be a fine accompaniment. If you're starting with fresh bread, spread the cubes on a baking sheet and dry them in a 350°F oven for about 10 minutes.

FRITTATA FOR ALL   MAKES 4 SERVINGS

2 teaspoons extra-virgin olive oil

⅓ cup thinly sliced Yukon Gold potatoes

½ cup chopped onion

Salt

6 large eggs

1 cup chopped fresh spinach

⅔ cup cubed stale bread (preferably from a baguette or rustic loaf)

5 cherry tomatoes

1   Preheat the oven to 400°F.

2   In an 8-inch cast-iron skillet, heat the olive oil over medium-high heat, tilting the pan to coat the bottom. Add the potatoes and cook, turning once, until lightly browned, 10 to 15 minutes total. Stir in the onion, sprinkle lightly with salt, and cook for another 3 to 4 minutes.

3   Meanwhile, in a large bowl, whisk the eggs well. Stir in the spinach, bread, tomatoes, and a few pinches of salt.

4   Pour the egg mixture into the skillet and cook for about 5 minutes, or until the eggs begin to set on the edges.

5   Transfer the pan to the oven and bake for 15 to 18 minutes, until the frittata puffs up a little and is firm to the touch. Let cool for a few minutes before cutting it into wedges. Serve hot or at room temperature.

HOSTING SUNDAY BRUNCH is one of my favorite things to do, and waffles are always on the menu. When my friend Guillermo told me he was experimenting with savory waffles, I thought it was a brilliant idea, and decided to play around with my own rendition. Here's what I came up with: a delicious cornbread waffle with jalapeño chile, Parmesan cheese, sun-dried tomatoes, and sage. It's subtle yet satisfying, and really good with the Curry-Tomato Omelet (page 28).

CORNBREAD WAFFLES WITH JALAPEÑOS AND SUN-DRIED TOMATOES

MAKES 5 OR 6 MEDIUM WAFFLES

1 cup all-purpose flour

1 cup finely ground yellow cornmeal

1 tablespoon sugar

2½ teaspoons baking powder

½ teaspoon salt

1½ cups milk (preferably whole)

2 large eggs

6 tablespoons butter, melted

½ cup freshly grated Parmesan cheese

2 tablespoons seeded and minced jalapeño

4 teaspoons minced, oil-packed sun-dried tomatoes

1 tablespoon minced fresh sage

Maple syrup, for serving

1 Preheat a Belgian waffle iron according to the manufacturer's instructions.

2 Measure the flour, cornmeal, sugar, baking powder, and salt into a large bowl, and whisk to combine. In a smaller bowl, whisk the milk, eggs, and melted butter. Pour the liquid ingredients into the dry mixture and stir with a large spoon or rubber spatula. The batter will be a little lumpy. Stir in the Parmesan, jalapeño, tomatoes, and sage. Using a handheld electric mixer on high speed, beat the batter until smooth, 1 to 2 minutes.

3 Cook the waffles using about ½ cup batter for each. Serve warm, with maple syrup on the side.

PACKED WITH PUMPKIN, apple cider, cinnamon, and nutmeg, these waffles are autumn on a plate. Serve them for brunch alongside Bacon with Brussels Sprouts and Apple Butter (page 157).

PUMPKIN-APPLE CIDER WAFFLES

MAKES 5 OR 6 MEDIUM WAFFLES

2 cups all-purpose flour

¼ cup sugar

1½ teaspoons baking powder

½ teaspoon ground cinnamon

½ teaspoon fleur de sel or other flaky sea salt

¼ teaspoon ground ginger

¼ teaspoon ground nutmeg

1 cup milk (preferably whole)

½ cup apple cider

¼ cup pumpkin puree

2 large eggs, separated

6 tablespoons butter, melted

1 teaspoon vanilla extract

Maple syrup, for serving

1   Preheat a Belgian waffle iron according to the manufacturer's instructions.

2   Measure the flour, sugar, baking powder, cinnamon, salt, ginger, and nutmeg into a large bowl. Whisk to combine. In a smaller bowl, whisk the milk, apple cider, pumpkin puree, egg yolks, melted butter, and vanilla until well combined. Pour the liquid ingredients into the dry mixture and mix well with a rubber spatula or large spoon.

3   In a medium bowl, beat the egg whites with a handheld electric mixer until they hold soft peaks, 3 to 4 minutes. (They should be softer than shaving cream but firmer than foam.) Using a rubber spatula, gently fold the egg whites into the batter until no streaks remain. Do not overmix or the egg whites will deflate.

4   Cook the waffles using about ½ cup batter for each. Serve warm, with maple syrup on the side.

THESE WAFFLES GET a nutritious boost from sweet potatoes and quinoa flour. Serve them with the equally healthful Curry Sautéed Kale (page 136).

SWEET POTATO BELGIAN WAFFLES MAKES 6 TO 8 MEDIUM WAFFLES

1 cup quinoa flour

¼ cup sugar

1½ teaspoons baking powder

½ teaspoon salt

1 cup whole milk or water

½ cup roasted and mashed sweet potato (about ½ large sweet potato)

2 large eggs, separated

4 tablespoons butter, melted, or coconut oil

1 teaspoon vanilla extract

Maple syrup or apple butter, for serving

1 Preheat a Belgian waffle iron according to the manufacturer's instructions.

2 Measure the flour, sugar, baking powder, and salt into a large bowl. Whisk to combine. In a smaller bowl, whisk the milk, mashed sweet potato, egg yolks, melted butter, and vanilla until well combined. Pour the liquid ingredients into the dry mixture and mix well.

3 In a medium bowl, beat the egg whites with a handheld electric mixer until they hold soft peaks, 3 to 4 minutes. Using a rubber spatula, gently fold the egg whites into the batter until no streaks remain. Do not overmix or the egg whites will deflate.

4 Cook the waffles using about ½ cup batter for each. Serve warm, with maple syrup or apple butter on the side.

SCORE! YOU'RE IN LUST. This special someone is hot for you, too—and is at your place for the night. This is not necessarily a love thing, but who cares? Skip dinner. Go straight to the sack. Feed your lover this combo as a midnight snack.

POTATOES AND PANCAKES (IT'S WHAT'S FOR BREAKFAST-DINNER)

MAKES 2 SERVINGS

FOR THE PANCAKES:

2 cups all-purpose flour

¼ cup sugar

2½ teaspoons baking powder

½ teaspoon salt

1½ cups milk (whole, skim, or nondairy)

2 large eggs

6 tablespoons butter, melted, plus 2 teaspoons for the pan

FOR THE POTATOES:

2 teaspoons extra-virgin olive oil

2 medium Yukon Gold potatoes, very thinly sliced

Salt

Freshly ground black pepper

Maple syrup, for serving

1 FOR THE PANCAKES: Measure the flour, sugar, baking powder, and salt into a large bowl. Whisk to combine. In a medium bowl, whisk the milk, eggs, and 6 tablespoons of melted butter until well combined. Pour the liquid ingredients into the dry mixture and mix with a large spoon or rubber spatula. Using a handheld electric mixer on high speed, beat the batter until smooth, 1 to 2 minutes. Set it aside while you cook the potatoes.

2 FOR THE POTATOES: Heat the oil in a 10-inch cast-iron skillet over medium-high heat, tilting the pan to coat the bottom. Add the potatoes in a single layer, sprinkle with a pinch of salt and a grind of pepper, and cook, undisturbed, until browned, about 3 minutes. Flip the potatoes over and cook the other side until deep golden brown, 2 or 3 more minutes.

3 While the potatoes cook, heat a crêpe pan or griddle over medium-high heat. Add the remaining 2 teaspoons butter, tilting the pan to coat the bottom. Cook the pancakes, using about ⅓ cup batter for each. When the top is bubbly and the bottom is golden brown (about 2 minutes), flip the pancakes. Cook until golden brown on the second side, about 2 minutes. Transfer to serving plates, along with the potatoes, and serve with maple syrup on the side.

THESE EXTRAVAGANT WAFFLES ARE a sensation at brunch, and they could even serve as a dinner-party dessert. If gluten is an issue for any of your guests, you can substitute gluten-free flour for the all-purpose.

CHOCOLATE WAFFLES WITH GANACHE
MAKES 9 OR 10 MEDIUM WAFFLES

1½ cups all-purpose flour

½ cup unsweetened cocoa powder

¼ cup sugar

2½ teaspoons baking powder

½ teaspoon salt

1½ cups milk (whole, skim, or nondairy)

2 large eggs

6 tablespoons coconut oil, melted

1 teaspoon vanilla extract

Chocolate Ganache, for serving (page 18)

1   Preheat a Belgian waffle iron according to the manufacturer's instructions.

2   Measure the flour, cocoa powder, sugar, baking powder, and salt into a large bowl. Whisk to combine. In a smaller bowl, whisk the milk, eggs, coconut oil, and vanilla. Pour the liquid ingredients into the dry mixture and use a large spoon or rubber spatula to mix. The batter will be slightly lumpy. Using a handheld electric mixer on high speed, beat the batter until smooth, 1 to 2 minutes.

3   Cook the waffles using about ½ cup batter for each. Serve warm, with chocolate ganache on the side.

BISCUITS ARE THE SOUTHERNER'S croissant. They're bready, buttery, and go great with jams and compotes, which I also adore. Plus, they're much quicker than anyone's croissant. This recipe takes only about 15 minutes to prepare and less than 25 minutes to bake. A post by my favorite Australian food blogger, Sarah Coates, inspired me to add the rosemary. If you don't have buttermilk on hand, you can substitute homemade sour milk: Just combine 1 tablespoon of lemon juice or distilled white vinegar with 1 cup of milk.

ROSEMARY-CHEDDAR BUTTERMILK BISCUITS WITH PEACH COMPOTE MAKES 8 OR 9 SMALL BISCUITS

2¼ cups all-purpose flour, plus more for dusting

2 teaspoons baking powder

½ teaspoon baking soda

¼ teaspoon salt

3½ ounces cheddar cheese, cut into small cubes and chilled

7 tablespoons butter, chilled

2 teaspoons minced fresh rosemary

1 cup plus 1 tablespoon buttermilk

Peach Compote, for serving (recipe follows)

1 Preheat the oven to 390°F. Line a baking sheet with parchment paper.

2 Measure the flour, baking powder, baking soda, and salt into a large bowl. Whisk to combine. Add the cheese, butter, and rosemary to the bowl and use your hands to mix the ingredients until you have pieces about the size of peas and grapes and the rest looks like clumps of sand. Add 1 cup of the buttermilk to the flour mixture and stir with a rubber spatula until the ingredients are just combined. Do not overmix or your biscuits will be tough.

3 Dust a work surface with flour and turn the dough out onto it. Working quickly, knead the dough just until it holds together, and form it into a ball. Press it flat and fold it over onto itself. Pat or roll it out to an even thickness of about 1½ inches or slightly more.

. . . continued

4   Use a 2½-inch biscuit cutter to cut as many biscuits as you can from the dough. Place them on the prepared baking sheet. Press the remaining dough together, pat it out to a 1½-inch thickness, and cut more biscuits. You should have 8 or 9 total. If there's any leftover dough, form it into a round and place it on the pan. Use your fingers or a pastry brush to smooth a little of the remaining 1 tablespoon buttermilk on top of each biscuit. (This will add a hint of shine.)

5   Bake the biscuits for 19 to 23 minutes, until golden brown and flaky. Allow them to cool for about 5 minutes before serving with Peach Compote. Be prepared for hot, melty cheese with each bite!

PEACH COMPOTE   MAKES ABOUT 1½ CUPS

I grew up in Georgia, so peaches are part of my heritage. They're also one of summer's best fruits. Compote is a great use for almost any kind of overripe, bruised fruit. Serve this with Rosemary-Cheddar Buttermilk Biscuits or plain yogurt. It keeps in an airtight container for up to 1 week in the refrigerator or 2 months in the freezer.

3 ripe peaches

1 cup water

1 teaspoon ground cinnamon

1 teaspoon sugar (optional)

1   Peel, pit, and chop the peaches and place them in a small saucepan.

2   Add the water, cinnamon, and sugar, if desired, and bring the mixture just to a boil over high heat. Adjust the heat to maintain a low simmer and cook until the peaches break down and the mixture thickens, 10 to 15 minutes. Allow it to cool slightly before serving, or refrigerate it in an airtight container for later use. The compote will keep for approximately 2 days.

REMEMBER THAT LUSH VERANDA in Andalusia we imagined back in the vegetable chapter? (See Fennel, Arugula, and Orange Zest Salad, page 141.) You're there again, and this time your host is serving dessert. I came up with this luscious, easy-to-make cake while playing around with gluten-free flour, but it works beautifully with all-purpose, too. Almond flour makes it extra moist, and, along with the orange blossom water (available at Middle Eastern and gourmet markets), transports you to the south of Spain. I serve the cake with crème fraîche and berries or with oranges, peels cut off and sliced into rounds strewn on top, but it's also lovely with a simple dusting of confectioners' sugar. Take the butter, eggs, and milk out of the refrigerator 30 minutes ahead to warm up so they can be incorporated more readily into the batter.

ORANGE BLOSSOM ALMOND CAKE MAKES 10 TO 12 SERVINGS

1   Preheat the oven to 350°F. Generously butter the bottom and sides of a 10-inch round cake pan. Cut a circle of parchment paper to fit the circumference of the pan bottom, butter both sides, and place it in the pan.

2   In a large bowl, use a wooden spoon to cream the butter and sugar until well blended, light, and fluffy. Add the eggs, one at a time, beating well after each addition. Stir in the milk, orange blossom water, and vanilla.

. . . *continued*

¾ cup (1½ sticks) butter, at room temperature, plus more for the pan

1 cup sugar

4 large eggs, at room temperature

½ cup whole milk, at room temperature

1 tablespoon orange blossom water (preferably Al Wadi brand)

1 teaspoon vanilla extract

1½ cups almond flour

½ cup all-purpose flour (or gluten-free, such as Cup4Cup)

2 teaspoons baking powder

½ teaspoon salt

Crème fraîche, for serving (optional)

Fresh raspberries, for serving (optional)

2 oranges, peels cut off and sliced into rounds (optional)

Confectioners' sugar, to dust the cake (optional)

3 In a medium bowl, whisk the flours, baking powder, and salt until well combined. Pour the dry ingredients into the wet ingredients and beat with a handheld electric mixer on medium speed until the batter is creamy, 1 to 2 minutes.

4 Spread the batter into the prepared pan and place it in the oven. Bake for about 30 minutes, or until the top is golden brown, the sides pull away from the pan, and a sharp knife inserted in the middle comes out clean.

5 Allow the cake to cool in the pan for 10 minutes before unmolding it. Serve warm or at room temperature, garnished with crème fraîche and raspberries, if desired. Or top the cake with the orange rounds, if desired. Another option is simply dusting it with confectioners' sugar. Leftover cake will keep, well wrapped in plastic, at room temperature for up to 4 days or in the freezer for up to 2 months. Thaw it in its wrapper at room temperature.

QUINOA FLOUR UPS THIS quick bread's nutritional quotient, and carrots, dill, feta, and sun-dried tomatoes give it a big flavor boost. Serve it with Curry-Carrot Soup (page 121) or swap it in for dinner rolls the next time you cook for friends. It also travels well in lunch bags and picnic baskets.

QUINOA QUICK BREAD WITH CARROTS AND DILL

MAKES 10 TO 12 THIN SLICES OR 8 THICK SLICES

Vegetable oil cooking spray

1 cup quinoa flour

½ cup all-purpose flour

3 large eggs

4 tablespoons butter, melted

2 tablespoons sour cream

2 teaspoons baking powder

½ teaspoon salt

½ cup chopped carrot

½ cup chopped fresh dill (feathery fronds only)

½ cup diced feta cheese

1 tablespoon chopped, oil-packed sun-dried tomatoes

1   Preheat the oven to 350°F. Coat a 5-by-9-inch loaf pan with vegetable oil cooking spray.

2   Add the flours, eggs, butter, sour cream, baking powder, and salt to a large bowl, stirring to combine. Beat with a handheld electric mixer on high speed until the batter is smooth, 2 to 3 minutes. Gently fold in the carrots, dill, feta, and tomatoes.

3   Pour the batter into the prepared pan and bake for about 40 minutes, or until the bread pulls away from the sides of the pan and a sharp knife inserted in the center comes out clean.

4   Set the pan on a rack to cool for about 10 minutes before unmolding the bread. Slice and serve warm or at room temperature. Store leftovers, wrapped in plastic, in the refrigerator for up to 1 week. It can also be frozen for up to 1 month as long as it's stored in an airtight container or wrapped tightly in plastic. Thaw the bread in its wrapper at room temperature, or discard the plastic wrap to toast slices lightly in an oven preheated to 350°F.

I DON'T HAVE AN ISSUE with gluten, but I have friends who do, and that was my motivation for creating this yummy chocolate-studded cake. The sour cream and almond flour make it extra moist and rich—perfect with tea.

GLUTEN-FREE CHOCOLATE CHIP CAKE

MAKES 10 TO 12 THIN SLICES OR 8 THICK SLICES

Vegetable oil cooking spray

¾ cup gluten-free flour
(such as Cup4Cup)

¾ cup almond flour

3 large eggs

⅓ cup sugar

¼ cup sour cream

¼ cup coconut oil

2 teaspoons baking powder

½ teaspoon salt

Grated zest of 1 lemon

1 cup semisweet chocolate chips

1   Preheat the oven to 350°F. Coat a 5-by-9-inch loaf pan with vegetable oil cooking spray.

2   In a large bowl, combine the flours, eggs, sugar, sour cream, coconut oil, baking powder, salt, and lemon zest. Beat with a handheld electric mixer on high speed until the batter is smooth, about 2 minutes. Use a rubber spatula to fold in the chocolate chips.

3   Pour the batter into the prepared pan and bake for about 40 minutes, or until the cake has pulled away from the pan and a sharp knife inserted into the center comes out clean.

4   Set the pan on a rack to cool for 10 minutes before unmolding the cake. Cut it into slices and serve warm or at room temperature. Leftover cake will keep, well wrapped in plastic, at room temperature for up to 4 days or in the freezer for up to 2 months. Thaw the cake in its wrapper at room temperature, or cut slices from the frozen loaf and lightly toast them in an oven preheated to 350°F.

LET ME SAY UP FRONT that this is the most demanding recipe in the book, but if you have basic baking skills, are feeling ambitious, and have at least 4 hours to spend in the kitchen, it's so worth it. It's a mash-up of my two favorite cakes. One is Gâteau Basque, from the Basque region of France, which I learned at Le Cordon Bleu. I love it because the exterior is crunchy while the interior is soft, with a layer of rum-spiked pastry cream and prunes. The other is a similar cake that I tasted in Rome at a chocolate shop called Said. Instead of prunes, it was filled with pastry cream and a layer of chocolate. It was one of the simplest, most delicious cakes I've ever had—ideal with tea or coffee. Speaking of which, the cake's name was inspired by an afternoon in Italy with my friends Patrick and Daniela. We were driving to the home of our mutual friend Ada, and I called her to say we were on the way. Ada, the most generous hostess ever, replied, "Oh, I'll put coffee on. Tell them they must stay for a cup." When I told Patrick, he said, "She's baking a cake. In Italy it's never a quick good-bye. And coffee means cake." Indeed it did. The most challenging part of this recipe is making the pastry cream, which requires copious whisking and total focus so you don't overcook the eggs. (If you've ever made a custard, you know the drill.) If you don't have a pastry bag, you can substitute a zip-top plastic bag, cutting a ½-inch opening in one corner after you have filled it. The cake will keep, wrapped well in plastic, in the refrigerator for up to 4 days or the freezer for up to 2 months.

LA DOLCE VITA CAKE

FOR THE PASTRY CREAM:

1 cup whole milk

1 vanilla bean, split lengthwise

2 large egg yolks

¼ cup granulated sugar

3 tablespoons cornstarch

3 tablespoons all-purpose flour

3 tablespoons Cointreau

FOR THE CHOCOLATE FILLING:

7 ounces dark chocolate

4 tablespoons butter

1 cup heavy whipping cream

2 large egg yolks

FOR THE CAKE:

10 tablespoons butter, at room temperature, cut into 10 pieces, plus more for the pan

2 cups all-purpose flour, plus more for the pan

3 large eggs

1½ cups confectioners' sugar, plus more for dusting

1½ teaspoons baking powder

1 tablespoon grated lemon zest

1 teaspoon vanilla extract

1 FOR THE PASTRY CREAM: Put the milk in a medium saucepan. Scrape the vanilla seeds from the bean into the milk and add the pod. Heat the milk over high heat, stirring, just until it boils. Set it aside off the heat and use a spoon to remove the vanilla bean pod. (You can rinse the pod, allow it to dry completely, and bury it in a container filled with granulated sugar to make vanilla sugar.)

2 In a medium bowl, whisk the egg yolks with the granulated sugar until thickened. In a small bowl, stir the cornstarch into the flour and whisk it into the egg yolk mixture until well combined.

3 Whisking constantly, slowly pour half of the hot milk into the egg mixture to temper it. Whisk the tempered mixture into the milk remaining in the saucepan and return it to the heat. Whisking constantly, heat the mixture over medium heat until it just comes to a hard boil. The mixture should be thick. Set it aside off the heat to cool for 5 minutes. Whisk in the Cointreau.

4 Cover a rimmed baking sheet with plastic wrap and spread the hot pastry cream onto it. Cover it with another layer of plastic wrap, pressing the plastic onto the pastry cream to prevent a skin from forming. Place the pan in the refrigerator until the pastry cream is completely cooled, 45 minutes to 1 hour.

5 FOR THE CHOCOLATE FILLING: While the pastry cream chills, make the chocolate filling. Chop the chocolate and butter and add them to the top of a double boiler or a stainless steel bowl set over a saucepan filled halfway with water. (The water should not touch

. . . continued

the bottom of the bowl.) Heat over medium heat, stirring after 5 minutes, until the chocolate and butter are melted and blended. Remove the double boiler top or bowl and set the chocolate mixture aside off the heat for 5 minutes to cool. Whisk in the cream and egg yolks and set aside.

6   FOR THE CAKE: Preheat the oven to 400°F. Butter and flour a 9-inch round cake pan, shaking off the excess flour.

7   Whisk the eggs in a small bowl and set aside, reserving 1 tablespoon of the egg in a small container to use as a wash.

8   In a large bowl, beat the butter pieces with the confectioners' sugar until the mixture is light and fluffy. Beat in the eggs until fully incorporated. In another bowl, sift the flour with the baking powder and beat the dry ingredients into the butter mixture, along with the lemon zest and vanilla. Use a rubber spatula to spread half of the cake batter in the prepared pan.

9   Transfer the cooled pastry cream to a pastry bag and pipe it out in concentric circles on top of the cake batter. Put 2 cups of the chocolate filling in another pastry bag and pipe it out in concentric circles on top of the pastry cream.

10   Fill a pastry bag with the remaining cake batter and pipe it out in concentric circles to cover the chocolate filling layer in the cake pan. Use a pastry brush to brush the top of the cake with the reserved beaten egg.

11   Bake the cake for 45 to 50 minutes, until it is a deep golden brown and firm to the touch. Set it on a rack to cool for 15 to 20 minutes. Cut it into wedges and serve warm or at room temperature, dusted with confectioners' sugar.

WHEN I LIVED IN FRANCE, my favorite chocolate wasn't remotely fancy. Packaged in brown paper like an old-school grocery bag, Nestlé Dessert Noir is a bar with zero aesthetic pretension. Printed on that wrapper was a simple recipe for a delicious chocolate mousse that was the starting point for this dessert. Note that it contains raw eggs. If that's a health concern, use pasteurized eggs and add 1½ teaspoons cream of tartar to the whites so they inflate properly.

SIMPLEST CHOCOLATE MOUSSE

MAKES 6 SERVINGS

7 ounces milk chocolate or semisweet chocolate

6 large eggs

Salt

1 Cut the chocolate into ½-inch pieces for even melting and put in a medium metal bowl. Set the bowl on top of a saucepan that's one-third to one-half full of water. (Or, if you have one, use a double boiler.) The water should not touch the bottom of the bowl. Heat the water over medium-high heat and stir the chocolate occasionally until it's completely melted.

2 Crack the eggs, placing the whites in one large bowl and the yolks in another. Add a pinch of salt to the whites. With a handheld electric mixer on high speed, beat the whites until they hold firm peaks, 2 to 3 minutes. Whisk the yolks until combined. Slowly add the melted chocolate to the yolks, whisking constantly, until well combined, about 2 minutes.

3 Using a rubber spatula, gently fold one-third of the whites into the chocolate mixture, taking care not to overmix so the eggs don't deflate. Fold in the remaining whites in two batches until just combined.

4 Divide the mousse among 6 ramekins that are approximately 4 inches in diameter. Refrigerate for at least 3 hours and as long as 8 hours before serving.

CLASSIC DONUTS ARE, of course, deep-fried, but I can't be bothered with the splattering oil and messy cleanup. Thankfully, there's such a thing as a donut pan (check out Amazon or Sur La Table), which allows you to bake your rings. The combination of salt, nutmeg, and cinnamon makes this baked version extra tasty. Plus, the recipe works well with gluten-free flour in place of all-purpose. If you don't have a pastry bag, put the batter in a large, plastic food-storage bag and cut a ½-inch opening in one corner.

BAKED DONUTS FOR YOUR FRIENDS
MAKES 12 TO 15 MEDIUM DONUTS

FOR THE DONUTS:

Vegetable oil cooking spray

2 cups all-purpose flour

¾ cup granulated sugar

2 teaspoons baking powder

1 teaspoon fleur de sel or coarse salt

1 teaspoon ground nutmeg

1 teaspoon ground cinnamon

¾ cup whole milk

2 large eggs, beaten

1 tablespoon butter, melted

1 teaspoon vanilla extract

1   FOR THE DONUTS: Preheat the oven to 325°F. Coat a donut pan or pans with vegetable oil cooking spray.

2   In a medium bowl, whisk the flour, sugar, baking powder, salt, nutmeg, and cinnamon to combine. In another bowl, whisk the milk with the eggs, melted butter, and vanilla. With a rubber spatula, stir the liquid ingredients into the flour mixture until just combined. (If you're using gluten-free flour, the batter will be very thick, but that's fine.)

3   Use a large spoon to scoop the batter from the bowl into a pastry bag and pipe it into the prepared pan, filling each donut cup two-thirds full.

4   Bake the donuts for 10 minutes. Remove the pan from the oven (close the oven door) and use a fork to snag each donut and turn it over. Return the pan to the oven and bake for 10 more minutes, or until the donuts are firm and lightly golden.

FOR THE GLAZE:

2 tablespoons hot water

1 cup confectioners' sugar

5 **FOR THE GLAZE:** Meanwhile, make the glaze by stirring the hot water into the confectioners' sugar in a shallow bowl.

6 Unmold the donuts onto a cooling rack. When cool enough to handle, dip each one into the glaze and set it back on the rack until the glaze is set. (Put wax paper under the rack to catch drips.) If you have leftover batter, let the pan cool to room temperature before baking the remaining batter in the same manner.

SANGRIA IS THE LEMONS-INTO-LEMONADE solution for leftover wine. This one came about when I combined some so-so white with Lillet, a citrusy aperitif wine, and Cointreau, a French brand of triple sec. A trip to the farmers' market yielded nectarines and cherries (I had mangoes in the fridge), and this festive quaff was born. I served it in a mason jar, and my friends were delighted—and a little buzzed. For a lighter version, swap out the white wine for ginger beer and skip the maple syrup.

MANGO-NECTARINE-CHERRY SANGRIA (FOR A PLEASANT BUZZ)

MAKES 3 SERVINGS

1 ripe mango, peeled, pitted, and sliced

1 nectarine, thinly sliced

1 cup white wine

½ cup Lillet Blanc

½ cup pitted and halved cherries

2 tablespoons Cointreau

Juice of ½ lime

½ teaspoon maple syrup

Ice cubes

Fresh mint leaves, for garnish

1 Combine the mango, nectarine, wine, Lillet, cherries, Cointreau, lime juice, and maple syrup in a large mason jar or other lidded container. Cover tightly and shake vigorously for a few seconds. Serve on the rocks in wine or cocktail glasses garnished with mint leaves.

THE HAPPY ENDING

"Have dessert but twice a week, but make it good and don't be afraid to eat it before the savories. Who's watching? Dessert is the reward for all of your good deeds."

—Indra Davis, friend and fellow dessert fan

My first food love was Mississippi mud pie. When I was little, my parents sometimes took me to the Chart House restaurant near New Haven, Connecticut, where we lived at the time. The only thing I ate happily on those outings was that chocolaty, layered, pudding-like pie. The thing is, desserts were rare in our house—my mom is an avidly healthy eater and cook who prefers Jane Brody to Betty Crocker—and I'm convinced that's one of the reasons I developed such a sweet tooth. At restaurants, I often ask for the dessert menu as soon as I sit down.

You could not imagine a better fairy tale for a dessert queen than spending a year at Le Cordon Bleu in Paris learning how to make the canon of French pâtisserie—everything from pâte à choux and éclairs to viennoiserie and chocolate truffles. My Francophile soul was overjoyed. Yet for all that lofty training, plus apprenticeships at a Parisian bakery and in Taillevent's three-star pastry kitchen, my favorite sweets remain simple, homey ones like Triple Chocolate Chip Cookies (page 203), Brownies (page 205), Ginger-Peach Crisp (page 194), and Rustic Strawberry Shortcake (page 196).

I'm also obsessed with making my own ice creams and sorbets (and I think everyone should invest in a $60 ice cream maker), so there are recipes for Milk Chocolate Sorbet (page 208)—the creamiest you can imagine—and Cantaloupe-Mint Sorbet (page 206). Sometimes the perfect happy ending is served in a glass, so you'll find a few fruit-based liqueurs, cocktails, and a sangria, too.

Some of the recipes yield single servings, and others make more. My thinking is this: If you're going to turn on the oven, why not make an extra serving or two for another day?

THE HAPPY ENDING RECIPES

I LOVE A LITTLE CRUNCH in my desserts and adore peaches and ginger, so creating this crumble was a natural one summer day when I found myself with a few too many ripe peaches. You could swap out peaches for apples or pears.

GINGER-PEACH CRISP (LE CRUMBLE) MAKES 1 SERVING

FOR THE TOPPING:

¼ cup old-fashioned rolled oats

3 tablespoons all-purpose flour

2 tablespoons butter, cut into small chunks and chilled

2 tablespoons sugar

1 teaspoon ground cinnamon

FOR THE FILLING:

2 peaches

¼ cup water

2 teaspoons sugar

1 teaspoon vanilla extract

1 teaspoon grated fresh ginger or minced crystallized ginger

1　Preheat the oven to 375°F.

2　FOR THE TOPPING: In a medium bowl, combine the oats, flour, butter, sugar, and cinnamon. Use your fingertips or a fork to work the butter into the dry mixture until it's crumbly. Set aside.

3　FOR THE FILLING: Peel, pit, and chop the peaches, and combine them in a small saucepan with the water, sugar, vanilla, and ginger. Bring the mixture to a boil over high heat. Decrease the heat to maintain a simmer and cook, covered, until the peaches soften and the mixture thickens, 8 to 10 minutes.

4　Pour the filling into a 4-inch ramekin and spoon the topping mixture evenly over it. Place the ramekin into the oven and bake for 15 to 20 minutes, until fragrant and light golden brown. Allow it to cool for 15 minutes before serving.

PERFECT FOR ONE and easily multiplied for guests, this is one of the simplest desserts ever. The first time I served it to friends, Omar's song "There's Nothing Like This" was playing in the background, and we all swooned over the fruit and the music. Ever since then, I've associated that song with this seductive concoction. Make this when strawberries are in season so they're full of flavor.

STRAWBERRIES WITH MASCARPONE (THERE'S NOTHING LIKE THIS)

MAKES 1 SERVING

⅓ cup heavy whipping cream

1 vanilla bean or 1 teaspoon vanilla extract

1 tablespoon mascarpone cheese, at room temperature

1 teaspoon confectioners' sugar, plus more as needed

6 fresh strawberries, hulled and halved

1 In a medium bowl, whisk the cream until soft peaks form, about 1 minute.

2 Cut the vanilla bean in half lengthwise and scrape the seeds into the cream (or add the vanilla extract). Add the mascarpone and confectioners' sugar and whisk gently to combine the ingredients. Taste and add more confectioners' sugar if desired.

3 Spoon the cream mixture into a pretty bowl and top with the strawberries. Serve immediately.

THIS TWIST ON A CLASSIC starts with a large cupcake for one and builds—up or out, as you prefer. The whipped cream adds a fluffy lightness and helps keep the layers stacked. It's almost too pretty to eat.

RUSTIC STRAWBERRY SHORTCAKE

MAKES 1 SERVING

FOR THE MINI CAKE:

2 tablespoons butter, melted, plus 1 teaspoon for the ramekin

¼ cup plus 1 teaspoon all-purpose flour

1 large egg white

2 tablespoons light brown sugar

1½ tablespoons whole milk

¼ teaspoon vanilla extract

¼ teaspoon baking powder

FOR THE WHIPPED CREAM:

⅓ cup heavy whipping cream

1½ teaspoons confectioners' sugar, plus more as needed

6 to 8 fresh strawberries, hulled and sliced

1 **FOR THE MINI CAKE:** Preheat the oven to 350°F. Use 1 teaspoon of the butter to grease the inside of a 4-inch ramekin. Add 1 teaspoon of the flour, rotating the ramekin to coat it evenly, and shake out the excess.

2 In a small bowl, whisk the egg white with the brown sugar until the sugar dissolves. Stir in the remaining ¼ cup flour and 2 tablespoons butter, the milk, vanilla, and baking powder, and beat until smooth.

3 Pour the batter into the prepared ramekin, set it on a baking sheet, and place it in the oven. Bake for 24 to 26 minutes, until the cake is golden on top and a toothpick inserted in the center comes out clean. Set it aside on a rack to cool completely, about 30 minutes.

4 **FOR THE WHIPPED CREAM:** In a medium bowl, whisk the cream until soft peaks form. Add the confectioners' sugar and whisk gently to combine. Taste and add more confectioners' sugar, if desired.

5 Remove the cake from the ramekin and cut it horizontally into two disks of cake of equal size. Place one disk on a dessert plate and top with half of the whipped cream and half of the strawberry slices. Stack the second disk on top and layer it with the remaining whipped cream and strawberries. Serve immediately.

WHEN I APPRENTICED at Taillevent in Paris, the pastry chef spiked his chestnut cakes with vintage rum. I prefer to drizzle them with melted chocolate or eat them with chocolate ice cream or Milk Chocolate Sorbet (page 208). The dense, rich consistency of these mini cakes may remind you of flourless chocolate cake—except they're less sweet. They keep well, so the recipe makes three. Wrap the extras tightly in plastic and stash them in the refrigerator for up to 4 days or in the freezer for up to 2 months for a ready-made treat when a friend drops by for coffee. Unwrap and pop them into a 350°F oven for 6 to 8 minutes before serving. Chestnut cream is a sweetened chestnut puree. It's available—as are candied chestnuts (*marrons glacés*)—from gourmet shops and online sources including amazon.com, which carries my favorite brand, Clément Faugier chestnut spread with vanilla.

PARISIAN MINI CHESTNUT CAKES

MAKES 3 SMALL CAKES

2 tablespoons butter, plus
1 teaspoon for the dish

1 cup chestnut cream

1 candied chestnut, diced (optional; preferred brand Clément Faugier)

2 large eggs

2 ounces bittersweet chocolate (optional)

1 Preheat the oven to 350°F. Use 1 teaspoon of the butter to grease three 3-inch ramekins or shallow tart molds.

2 In a small saucepan, melt the remaining 2 tablespoons butter over medium heat. Let cool slightly.

3 In a medium bowl, whisk the chestnut cream, melted butter, and candied chestnut, if desired, until well combined. Add the eggs, one at a time, whisking after each addition.

. . . continued

4   Place the prepared ramekins on a baking sheet and divide the batter evenly among them. Place the pan in the oven and bake the cakes for 30 to 35 minutes, until firm and lightly browned. Set aside on a rack to cool for 10 minutes before unmolding.

5   Meanwhile, chop the chocolate, if using, into ½-inch pieces and add it to the top of a double boiler or a metal bowl set on top of a saucepan that's half full of water. (The water should not touch the bottom of the bowl.) Heat over medium-high heat, stirring after 5 minutes, until the chocolate is completely melted.

6   To serve, unmold a cake onto a dessert plate and drizzle with the melted chocolate. Serve warm. (Or eat it straight from the ramekin!)

AT THE HEIGHT OF fig season in France, the pastry chef I worked for at Taillevent sautéed the succulent fruit in butter with rosemary and honey and served them with goat cheese ice cream. I use butter, sugar, and cinnamon for this ultra-simple dessert and serve it over vanilla ice cream, though it's also yummy on its own. Make it when California figs are in season in June and July and again from August through October.

SAUTÉED FIGS

MAKES 1 SERVING

1 tablespoon butter

1½ teaspoons sugar

1 teaspoon ground cinnamon

6 fresh figs, halved

Vanilla ice cream, for serving

1   In a skillet, melt the butter over medium heat, tilting the pan to coat the bottom. Mix the sugar with the cinnamon and sprinkle the mixture over the butter. Place the fig halves in the pan, cut side down.

2   Use a spoon or spatula to move the figs around until they are coated in the butter mixture. Let them cook until somewhat caramelized, 1 to 2 minutes, making sure the sugar doesn't burn.

3   Remove the pan from the heat, spoon the figs over a scoop of vanilla ice cream, and enjoy.

I CONSIDER MYSELF THE original cookie monster, and my all-time favorite is chocolate chip. I add cocoa powder to the dough, use both semisweet and milk chocolate morsels, and add a little more salt than usual to bring out all that chocolaty goodness. If you like yours less salty, use 1½ teaspoons salt instead of 2. This is a cookie-on-demand recipe: You bake as many as you want upfront, and form the rest of the dough into a slice-and-bake roll to stash in your freezer.

TRIPLE CHOCOLATE CHIP COOKIES

MAKES ABOUT 3 DOZEN 3- TO 3½-INCH COOKIES

2 cups all-purpose flour

3 tablespoons unsweetened cocoa powder

2 teaspoons fleur de sel or other flaky sea salt

1 teaspoon baking soda

1½ cups lightly packed light brown sugar

1 cup (2 sticks) butter, at room temperature

1 teaspoon vanilla extract

2 large eggs

1 cup semisweet chocolate chips

1 cup milk chocolate chunks

1 Preheat the oven to 375°F.

2 In a medium bowl, whisk the flour with the cocoa powder, salt, and baking soda until well combined.

3 In a large bowl, use a wooden spoon or handheld electric mixer to beat the brown sugar and butter until well combined and creamy. Beat in the vanilla. Add the eggs, one at a time, mixing after each addition. Add the dry ingredients, mixing until combined. Stir in the semisweet and milk chocolate pieces.

4 Decide how many cookies you would like to eat right now and drop that many heaping teaspoons of dough onto an ungreased baking sheet, spacing them at least 2 inches apart. (For the remaining dough, see step 6.)

. . . continued

5   Bake the cookies for 9 to 11 minutes, until firm and lightly golden. Let them cool on the baking sheet for a few minutes before transferring them to a cooling rack. Serve warm.

6   Cut a 20-inch piece of wax or parchment paper and dump the remaining dough onto it. Using your hands and the natural curl of the paper, roll the dough into a log shape about 1½ inches in diameter. Wrap the dough log tightly in aluminum foil or plastic wrap and place it in the freezer.

7   Whenever you want cookies, preheat the oven to 375°F, unwrap one end of the dough log, and cut a 1-inch slice for each cookie. Place on an ungreased baking sheet and bake for about 10 minutes, or until lightly golden. Rewrap and refreeze the remaining dough. It will keep well in the freezer for up to 2 months.

COOKING IS MY FAVORITE way to unwind, but going to the movies is a close second, and Chiwetel Ejiofor is my biggest screen crush. I've adored him since *Dirty Pretty Things* and *Love Actually*, and can be insufferable on the subject of the masterpiece that is *Kinky Boots*. I once read in an interview that he loves brownies, which means we have a shared passion. Chiwetel, this one's for you. For a big dollop of indulgence, spoon a little vanilla ice cream on top.

BROWNIES FOR CHIWETEL

MAKES 2 SERVINGS

3 tablespoons butter, plus more for dish

½ cup semisweet chocolate chips

¼ cup sugar

1 large egg

1 teaspoon vanilla extract

1 teaspoon fleur de sel or other flaky sea salt

1 tablespoon all-purpose flour

1 Preheat the oven to 350°F. Butter two 4-inch ramekins.

2 In a small saucepan, combine the chocolate chips and butter and let them melt, stirring occasionally, over low heat. Let the mixture cool for 5 minutes.

3 In a medium bowl, whisk the sugar and egg until well combined. Still whisking, gradually pour in the cooled chocolate mixture, vanilla, and salt. Add the flour and stir until just combined. Do not overmix.

4 Pour the batter into the prepared ramekins, set them on a baking sheet, and place in the oven. Bake for 20 to 24 minutes, until firm.

5 Allow the brownies to cool until the middle solidifies, 10 to 15 minutes, before serving.

IT WAS SWELTERINGLY HOT and I had an abundance of melon and mint, so I thought, why not make sorbet? Nectar of the gods—that's what this stuff is. It's reason enough to buy an ice cream maker.

CANTALOUPE-MINT SORBET

MAKES 1 PINT

1 cup water

½ cup sugar

1⅔ cups diced ripe cantaloupe (about ½ large cantaloupe)

1 tablespoon chopped fresh mint

1 Make a simple syrup by combining the water and sugar in a small saucepan over low heat, stirring occasionally until all the sugar dissolves. Set it aside to cool.

2 Put the cantaloupe in a blender along with the cooled simple syrup and mint. Pulse a few times to mix, then process on high speed until smooth and homogenous. Pour the puree into a bowl, cover, and refrigerate until well chilled, at least 2 hours.

3 Pour the cold mixture into an ice cream maker and process it according to the manufacturer's instructions. Serve immediately, or transfer to a covered container and store in the freezer for up to 1 week.

IN THE OTTO PREMINGER FILM *Bonjour Tristesse* (which translates as "Hello, Sadness"), the main character, Cecile, has ice cream for breakfast. I love that idea, and have been known to eat this sublime sorbet in the morning with raspberries. It's better for dessert, though. This recipe is inspired by a dark chocolate frozen treat from David Lebovitz. Have a few scoops on a hot summer's night sprinkled with fleur de sel or cinnamon.

MILK CHOCOLATE SORBET (BONJOUR HAPPINESS)   MAKES 1½ PINTS

¾ cup unsweetened Dutch-process cocoa powder

½ cup sugar

2¼ cups water

5 ounces milk chocolate, finely chopped

1 teaspoon vanilla extract

1   In a 3-quart saucepan, whisk the cocoa powder and sugar into 1¼ cups of the water. Bring the mixture just to a boil over high heat, whisking constantly. Remove the pan from the heat.

2   Add the milk chocolate and vanilla and stir until the chocolate melts completely. Stir in the remaining 1 cup water. Using a handheld electric mixer, beat the mixture on high speed for 30 seconds. Scrape it into a clean container and refrigerate, covered, until well chilled, at least 2 hours.

3   Pour the cold mixture into an ice cream maker and process it according to the manufacturer's instructions. Serve immediately, or transfer to a covered container and store in the freezer for up to 1 week.

EVERY HOSTESS AND HOST should know how to make a favorite cocktail for guests. Mine is Kir, named for Félix Kir, a longtime mayor of Dijon who popularized the drink after World War II. All over France, this vivid red, sweetly refreshing combination of crème de cassis and white wine serves as a kind of punctuation, marking the end of the workday and the transition to evening. Mayor Kir's bartender would have made it with Aligoté, a white wine from Burgundy, but I use Chardonnay. When I feel festive, I make it a Kir Royale by substituting Champagne or another sparkling white wine.

YOU NEED A COCKTAIL: KIR

MAKES 1 SERVING

1 tablespoon crème de cassis

6 ounces Chardonnay

1 Pour the crème de cassis into a wineglass and top it off with the wine. Serve.

BE PATIENT; THIS IS going to take a while, but it's so worth it. Concocting liqueurs—distilled spirits made from a base of liquor and sugar combined with fruit, herbs, or spices—is a great do-it-yourself project. A trip to your farmers' market can feed your imagination. I love strawberries, so when summer begins, they're the fruit I play with most. Add a tablespoon of this liqueur to Champagne or Prosecco for a simple summer cocktail. Or pour 2 shots of it over ice cubes in a rocks glass, and finish it with the juice of half a lime and a few shredded mint leaves.

KLANCY'S STRAWBERRY LIQUEUR   MAKES 1 PINT

3 cups fresh strawberries, rinsed, hulled, and halved

2 cups vodka

¼ cup sugar

1   In a clean 32-ounce mason jar or similar-size lidded glass container, combine the strawberries, vodka, and sugar. Close the lid tightly and shake well to dissolve the sugar. Store the jar in the refrigerator for 3 weeks, shaking it every few days.

2   Use a slotted spoon to remove the strawberries (serve them with ice cream for a fast dessert). The liqueur will keep in the refrigerator for up to 3 months.

THIS SENSATIONAL SANGRIA IS summer in a glass, the ideal lubricant for a warm-weather party. Just multiply the ingredients by the number of guests.

WATERMELON SANGRIA MAKES 2 SERVINGS

1 cup chopped watermelon

1 cup rosé wine

½ cup Lillet Blanc

2 tablespoons Cointreau

Juice of ½ lime

½ teaspoon maple syrup

1 Combine the watermelon, wine, Lillet, Cointreau, lime juice, and maple syrup in a blender. Pulse briefly to mix and then process on high speed until the watermelon is liquefied. Serve immediately in wine or cocktail glasses.

WHEN I SEE SUMMER cherries at the farmers' market, I can't resist; they're too pretty not to buy. After polishing off a few handfuls, I usually begin thinking about other ways to consume them, and that's how I came up with this luscious liqueur. Inexpensive vodka is just fine for this recipe. For the freshest cherries, look for green, supple stems. After they've macerated in the liqueur for three weeks, enjoy the boozy cherries over vanilla ice cream.

KLANCY'S CHERRY LIQUEUR

MAKES 1 PINT

1 pint sweet cherries

2 cups vodka

¼ cup sugar

1 Stem and pit the cherries and cut the flesh in half.

2 In a 32-ounce mason jar or similar-size lidded glass container, combine the cherries, vodka, and sugar. Close the lid tightly and shake well to dissolve the sugar. Store the jar in the refrigerator for 3 weeks, shaking it every few days.

3 Use a slotted spoon to remove the cherries after three weeks (serve the cherries with whipped cream or ice cream for a quick dessert). The liqueur will keep in the refrigerator for up to 3 months.

THIS COCKTAIL IS NAMED for *Cherry Bombe*, a gorgeous magazine that celebrates women in food—and, fittingly, it stars my beloved cherry liqueur. For a lighter version, skip the Cointreau.

CHERRY BOMBE (A COCKTAIL ODE TO MY FAVORITE MAGAZINE) MAKES 1 SERVING

½ cup Prosecco or other sparkling white wine

2 tablespoons Klancy's Cherry Liqueur (page 213)

1 tablespoon Cointreau

1 Pour the Prosecco, cherry liqueur, and Cointreau into a coupe glass and stir with a cocktail spoon. Drink immediately.

INDEX

———————

"Tu t'aimes bien."